PRAISE FOR
A VIEW FROM THE BALCONY

Gary De Carolis skillfully blends his wide ranging personal history with conceptual understandings of the idea of leadership in complex environments. His passion for the people he has served comes through clearly in the context of the complexities of governmental policy and human nature in our communities. This was a treat to read and will be helpful, particularly to younger administrators, who are looking for ways to be more effective leaders on behalf of the people they serve.

Gary De Carolis's clear and conversational down-home approach to leadership and all of its aspects . . . gently pulls the reader to a good place.

—Cornelius Hogan, previous Secretary of Vermont's Agency of Human Services and coauthor of *At the Crossroads: The Future of Health Care in Vermont*

This book, particularly the "lessons learned" chapter, is an important and critical resource for those states, tribes, and communities that are building systems of care for those who often do not have a voice—our children.

—Ethleen Iron Cloud-Two Dogs, Project Director, Nagi Kicopi (Calling the Spirit Back), Wakanyeja Pawicayapi, Inc. (The Children First)

This is a very honest look at the hard work and leadership that it takes to do systems change work, especially for parents and families. It also shows that it is all worth it!

—TJ Rosenberg, parent advocate, Las Vegas, NV

This much-needed book provides a unique historical perspective of the system of care movement. In it, De Carolis provides a powerful road map for community organizers who are collaborating to improve the lives of youth with emotional-behavioral disorders and their families. Leaders, case managers, and families in every community that is moving forward to coordinate children's mental health services will be inspired to see the potential in every child and informed in ways that will enhance their own system of care. This book is must reading for anyone considering how to develop a new system of care and for established collaborative members who want to renew their commitment to coordinated, meaningful care for their children.

—Michael Furlong, PhD, Professor, University of California, Santa Barbara

A VIEW FROM THE BALCONY

A VIEW FROM THE BALCONY

LEADERSHIP CHALLENGES IN SYSTEMS OF CARE

GARY DE CAROLIS

Foreword by Ronald Heifetz, MD and Marty Linsky
Coauthors, *Leadership on the Line*

For information, please contact:

Brown Books Publishing Group
16200 North Dallas Parkway, Suite 170
Dallas, Texas 75248
www.brownbooks.com
972-381-0009

ISBN 1-933285-05-2
LCCN 2005926882
2 3 4 5 6 7 8 9 10

To my daughters:

Emily Grace, Alina Katherine, and Sophie Jane

TABLE OF CONTENTS

ACKNOWLEDGMENTS

This book would have not been possible without the dedication, persistence, and remarkable editing ability of my friend and colleague Anne Lezak. She consistently encouraged me to put down on paper what I wanted to say and then went about the job of making those words understandable for the reader. Thank you, Anne, for all you have done to make this book move from an idea and lifelong hope to the reality of seeing it in print today.

My friend and colleague Kenley Wade was always there in the beginning to encourage me to keep writing so that others could benefit from the many lessons that he listened to day after day as I plugged away at the manuscript. Little did he realize the importance of his ears to my early writings.

Gabrielle Barnhart was so willing to do whatever it took to make sure that my collection of writing someday ended up in publication. She retyped whole chapters of the book and always had an encouraging word to keep me going. Everyone should have such a wonderful cheerleader for the most important endeavor in their profession. Thanks, Bob Lazun, for your steady light during the three years of writing. Jenny Rodgers generously read the Navajo story and offered helpful input. Long before there was even a thought of writing this book, Jenny was so kind to take me to homes and places in the Navajo Nation that I might better understand and appreciate the heart and soul of the Navajo people. I will never forget those precious journeys through canyons, deserts, and plains, only to be overshadowed by the generous and soulful Navajo people, who opened their homes and hearts to me.

A big thank-you to Marty Linsky and Ronald Heifetz, who have articulated a theory of leadership that organized my experiences into a framework that made my years of leadership and system change finally understandable to me. Their body of work has aided thousands of others, including those working to more effectively help communities that want to ensure an optimum life for children with disabilities. "A View from the Balcony" is an important metaphor used by Heifetz and Linsky in their teaching regarding the leader's perspective. I am grateful for their permission to use it as part of the title for this book.

My deep appreciation for all my Vermont colleagues who offered me a chance to help plan and implement one of the nation's best systems of care for children and families. A special "thank you" to Rod Copeland and John Pierce for their unending trust in my abilities to make it all happen. This book could not have been possible without your support of my leadership.

The team at Brown Publishing has my deepest gratitude for a job well done. They were incredible in taking my well-intended manuscript and making it shine.

FOREWORD

Leading deep change in any system, in any organization, community, group, or family, what we call adaptive leadership, is difficult and dangerous work. That's why we, and you, don't do it more often.

But leading deep change on behalf of deeply held values and beliefs gives human lives meaning and purpose. That's why all of us would like to do it more than we do.

Scholars and practitioners of leadership spend a lot of time, too much time, in our view, on the inspirational aspects of exercising leadership. The importance of this book, and of Gary De Carolis's professional journey, lies in the focus on the "perspirational" aspects of leadership. In that sense, the usefulness of this book goes beyond the world of children with emotional and mental health issues to anyone seeking to exercise adaptive leadership.

For the two of us, as teachers and consultants about leadership, what gives meaning and purpose to our lives is being able to provide useful intellectual and tactical guidance and support for those who are doing the hard work out there in their communities.

This book documents a powerful example of that, of the

fusion of passion and commitment with ideas about leadership and behaviors for the hard-nosed application of those ideas, for the purpose of making real progress by leading significant change.

From our perspective, it is no accident that Gary began to develop his leadership insights, and then capacity, in the intense and tumultuous world of local politics. There is a paradox about leadership and politics in a democratic setting. On the one hand, democratic politics are designed to discourage leadership and to encourage pandering to constituencies of one kind or another. On the other hand, democratic politics are also designed so that in order to get anything important done, practitioners have to employ many of the behaviors that are central to leadership, for challenging rather than pandering to constituencies.

Here are two examples of the behaviors we are talking about, taken from Gary's experience as told in these pages: separating role from self, and the insight that follows personal attacks are usually best understood as attacks on the ideas or issues or threat you represent to the attacker. Responding to the pressure to answer the attack personally serves to collude with the attacker in moving the conversation off the issue. Or, for another example, in the role of the authority person, exercising leadership often requires resisting the temptation to solve problems for people and take the issues off their shoulders. Instead, leadership often means creating what we call a "holding environment," a safe place where you can give the work back to people and orchestrate the conflict among them rather than resolve it.

Gary's story also illustrates another critical reality about exercising leadership: the need to take care of self. Exercising leadership is draining, emotionally and physically. Success and survival require that you pay attention to what is happening to you and that you find time for reflection and distance. You need sanctuaries, and confidants.

Gary De Carolis flatters us by attributing some of his success to his using the ideas we teach and by asking us to contribute this foreword to his story. But he honors us, as well as all the families who have benefited by his leadership, by the good he has done in applying those ideas to the challenges of making progress in systems of care for children with disabilities.

Marty Linsky and Ronald Heifetz, MD
Coauthors, *Leadership on the Line: Staying Alive through the Dangers of Leading;* coprincipals, Cambridge Leadership Associates (www.cambridge-leadership.com); and faculty, John F. Kennedy School of Government, Harvard, Cambridge, MA, January 2005

INTRODUCTION

This book is an accumulation of twenty years of experience designing, building, and administering systems of care for children experiencing a serious emotional disturbance and their families. What started in the mid-1980s as a small federal grant program to help states begin conceptualizing what an ideal children's mental health system could look like has become a national movement. The goal is quite simple, actually: to ensure that children with multiple needs can receive the necessary services and supports within their homes and communities. Fortunately for me, I've ridden the crest of this social reform movement for all of those years, first in Vermont, then in Washington DC, heading the very branch that gave Vermont its first grant in 1985, and now leading a consulting firm targeting leadership and policy issues in community-based systems for children and their families.

System reform, the thing that attracted me to this work those many years ago, is actually the most difficult aspect. Back in 1985, when we new and ambitious agents of change began helping our respective states explore what the ideal children's mental health system could look like, it seemed so easy. We weren't necessarily changing anything at that early stage;

we were dreaming about what could be for our children and families. Sure, there were signs of the struggles that lay ahead. Some of the grant directors actually did propose changes based on the early feedback from parents and providers; that usually resulted in swift and dire consequences for them. Some were intentionally isolated and some were dismissed. A small number were able to begin making some changes with the support of forward-thinking allies within state departments of mental health and other child-serving agencies.

The most rewarding part of that early work was being part of a network of enthusiastic, hopeful grant directors all across the country, sharing the excitement of designing systems of care built around some basic principles that we all seemed to agree upon. Principles like family involvement, cultural competence, interagency collaboration, child-centered care, and home and community-based services drove our work. Later, the principles of accountability and strength-based approaches to developing plans of care for children and families were added.

Those principles galvanized all of us as a group of project directors. Beyond that, they spoke powerfully to many parents and service providers in our home states. Together, we were becoming a force to be reckoned with for a new way of serving children all across the country. We were openly challenging the current belief system that children with challenging behaviors and diagnoses should be removed from their homes and communities and sent off to institutions for the good of everyone. We were architects and designers with a passion to build systems that we hoped would change how America served the mental health needs of its children. As a colleague of mine put it, we were "public entrepreneurs."

The excitement for the work was intoxicating to many of us, and we didn't give much thought to those early difficulties of some of our colleagues whose hopes for change were dashed once they tried to put their grand proposals into practice. However, in time we would all understand what was happening to them. As the design work of the '80s moved to the implementation work of the '90s, shifts began to occur.

In 1988, the Robert Wood Johnson Foundation invested over $20 million to help determine whether the system-of-care designs being touted would truly make a difference for children with serious emotional disturbance. Seven sites were chosen to do the work of actually building local systems of care based on the system-of-care principles.

The good news was that four years later, when the data were compiled, they clearly showed that for children who had a serious emotional disturbance, providing a range of services and supports within their homes and communities made a measurable positive difference. The bad news was that getting these systems of care on line meant mightily upsetting the status quo. It meant that therapists who were comfortable with fifty-minute office sessions might now have to do some of their work in schools and homes. It meant agencies opening their doors to parents to let them participate in meetings that heretofore had been the exclusive domain of the professional world. It meant proposals to blend funds among agencies, and sharing data across agencies. And it meant that the practice of sending children to out-of-state facilities was now going to be challenged; an emerging protocol that required creating the capacity for these same children to receive services in their homes and communities through individualized plans of care would replace it. In the end, it meant system change with all its inherent struggles.

As recently as 1992, when the Robert Wood Johnson Foundation program ended, only a few of us recognized what an enormous task lay ahead for any community that embarked on such an ambitious plan of system change. As one of those who had been involved from the beginning and played a central role in both designing and implementing Vermont's new system of care for children experiencing serious emotional disturbance and their families, I understood the challenge on both a professional and personal level.

I was fortunate to be chosen for a federal job that ideally positioned me to share what we learned in Vermont. In 1993, I became the chief of the Child, Adolescent and Family Branch within the federal Center for Mental Health Services. This branch had just been given the lead responsibility to manage a new congressionally authorized program built on the success of the Robert Wood Johnson Foundation effort.

First authorized in 1992 and appropriated $4.9 million dollars, the Comprehensive Community Mental Health Services for Children and Their Families Program today has surpassed a $100 million annual appropriation. Over eighty communities, states, Indian tribes, and US territories have now received major, multiyear federal grant funding to put the system-of-care principles into practice. While the projects can boast of many lasting and proud achievements on behalf of their children and their families, the bumps and bruises experienced within the grant communities have also been significant.

We soon discovered that very few people receiving the grants from the federal government were prepared for the kind of resistance they would face when they began the work of creating new systems of care. The "architects" had now handed the work over to the "engineers"! Unfortunately, many of the communities receiving grant funding had not had the advantage of the much more modest grants in the 1980s that allowed for the architectural work. Further, few if any of the new grant communities were trained in the engineering aspects of building a system of care.

The work began, and many of the problems we feared would soon surface. In retrospect, it is amazing how few truly understood the hard work that would be required to build an effective, responsive, sustainable system of care. While a number of mental health experts had written respected articles and even books about what should comprise a system of care, none of those writers had actually done the work. Their approaches were therefore more theoretical than practical in nature. It was important back in the 1980s as it is even now to have the conceptual basis for building systems of care, but there was little guidance provided about the hard realities of implementation.

All players were eager to share in the apparent financial benefits of the generous federal grants, but few were ready to embrace the concepts that underlay the infusion of new funds. Community mental health centers and other major players resisted the changes. Parents were hired by agencies and soon fired for advocating primarily for the interests of families and lacking in business acumen. Providers had no concept of cultural competence and hired staff that had little understanding of the population of children and families they were about to serve. Local family organizations could not relate to their statewide family organization because of the cultural differences and the more operational aspects of their local system-building work. Departments of mental health circled the wagons around the new funds secured from the grants and pulled back from interagency collaborative efforts. Directors of projects were fired as they began to push against the status quo to implement the system changes that were both promised and required through the grant projects. And this is just a small sampling of the upheaval and difficulties faced by the grant communities.

In fact, it is safe to say that if you are doing the work of building your system of care, then both "you" as a leader, and "you" as a community will experience much stress and disruption as you create this new way of carrying out the business of serving children in their homes and communities. If a community has not experienced much difficulty, then it is probably not doing real system change work.

Realizing how very hard this system change work was going to be, we in the Child, Adolescent and Family Branch supplemented the grants with a number of activities to provide support and technical assistance to grant communities. We provided opportunities for grantees to share their successes and challenges with one another in virtual learning communities and through twice-yearly grantee meetings. We contracted for a series of "promising practice" monographs on various aspects of system-of-care work. We offered intensive weeklong leadership academies for parent and professional leader duos in the grant communities so they could better understand their shared leadership roles. We sponsored policy academies to help communities understand the critical role of policy development as a way to help sustain the work begun with the federal funding.

This book is a natural follow-up to my years of work on behalf of systems of care for children with special needs and their families. It is all about that process of going from architect to engineer. It is written by someone who has had the wonderful honor of working within communities and also being able to support communities as they have strived mightily to make the world a better place for their children who have mental health challenges. For all the difficulties that ensue from such an effort, it is the right thing to do. My hope is that this book will help move communities closer to their collective dream of having all of their children served within their homes and communities. As the great migrant worker organizer César Chávez pointed out, "It is not enough to progress as individuals while our friends and neighbors are left behind."

It must be remembered that there is nothing more difficult to plan, more doubtful of success, nor more dangerous to manage than the creation of a new system.

For the initiator has the enmity of all who would profit by the preservation of the old institutions and merely lukewarm defenders in those who would gain by the new ones.

—*Machiavelli,* The Prince *(1513)*

CHAPTER ONE:

BUILDING
A FOUNDATION
FOR SYSTEMS
OF CARE

*Don't ever take a fence down until
you know why it was put up.*

—*Robert Frost*

A Short History

The history of our country as it relates to serving people with disabilities would suggest that communities cannot care for all their citizens. If you have a disability you need to be served outside of your community in institutions, sometimes far from home: this was the prevailing attitude and social policy up to the mid-1960s and it persists even today in some parts of the country.

The model of creating separate institutions for people with disabilities dates back to the early 1800s. This approach was premised on the notion that if we move people with special needs into a place that provides both housing and the support services they need, we can efficiently serve them and lift their quality of life. However, a review of the history of institutions for people with developmental disabilities and those with mental illness demonstrates that this lofty goal was rarely realized. Conditions of overcrowding, poor nourishment for the patients, and lack of attention and care, often to the point of neglect, were more the norm.

When I was a small boy in New Jersey in the 1950s, my father occasionally took me along to the New Jersey Neuro-psychiatric Institute in Skillman, where he worked as a music therapist. I will never forget walking down the basement halls with him and seeing cages line one side of the hallway. The cages were filled with straw that served as beds for patients, who were lying naked on the floor. Shocking!

It has been a shameful American tradition to isolate and remove those groups of people who are "different." We need go no further than the segregation of African-Americans, Native Americans, and, at times, Asian-Americans to see our approach to dealing with differences. Is it any wonder that people with disabilities would have the same fate?

The other powerful separator in our country has been class. Even our nation's capital today in many ways typifies how we live in community. Southeast Washington DC, houses overwhelmingly poor and African-American people, and Northwest Washington typically houses the white and upper-class. We can do better.

To further illustrate this issue of segregation, in rural Boyds, Maryland, there sits a one-room schoolhouse that served as the primary school for African-American children in the early part of the twentieth century. Across the street is a more modern brick building that was, for years, the high school for African-American youth of the community. With the advent of integration in the late 1950s and early 1960s, both schools were abandoned. Guess what group of young people moved into the African-American high school? Children with disabilities. That school moved from serving one segregated group of young people to another. We can do better.

Expanding Opportunities for Children with Special Needs: PL 94-142

We have made some important steps in the right direction. In 1975, a piece of landmark federal legislation was passed that significantly expanded opportunities for children with disabilities. Public Law 94-142, the Education for Handicapped Children Act (renamed in 1990 the Individuals with Disabilities Education Act), requires that all children with disabilities be provided a free and appropriate education in the least restrictive environment no matter what their level of disability. This meant that children finally had the legal right to stay within their homes and communities rather than be shipped off to institutions, often for years at a time.

The law was built on the backs of parents of children with disabilities who stood up and said, "We want to have our children live at home and attend schools in our communities." The passage of PL 94-142 showed the power of parents coming together for a common purpose. It was the beginning of the drumbeat for communities caring for all their children.

As significant an achievement as the passage of legislation outlawing segregation of children based on disability was, it is clear that passing a law and implementing it are two very different activities. The extent to which states changed their policies and practices in response to the new federal law varied wildly. In Vermont, for example, long one of the top states for including children with disabilities in the regular classroom, a vigorous effort was made to comply with the principles of PL 94-142. The result is that today, in the neighborhood of 80 percent of children with disabilities are included in regular classrooms.

On the other side of the scale, until recently, a Southern state had a director of special education for over twenty years whose mantra was that she was not going to implement special education no matter what federal laws were on the books. In education, as with building systems of care, achieving social reform of any kind is very difficult and can take many years.

Public Law 94-142 clearly stepped up the pressure to serve children with special needs within their home communities. It opened the door for all groups of children with special needs and their parents to articulate that they wanted services provided within the context of home and community. As far as children who had a serious emotional disturbance were concerned, the new law gave them legal standing but fell short of making sure they were supported within their home schools.

THE PROMISE OF PL 94-142
AND THE REALITY

As a Vermont director of special education once said, "Children with serious emotional disturbance are the last group the law has been able to support, and as we turn our attention to these children there is no money to do anything for them." While the federal commitment was to be at 40 percent of the cost of services, in reality PL 94-142 is funded at only 16.7 percent (Council, 2002) of the cost of serving children with disabilities. The lack of federal financial support coupled with the lack of understanding of the programmatic needs of children with mental health disorders means that far too many children continue to be served in out-of-community placements, if they are identified and served at all.

Why should this be so, given the clear mandate of PL 94-142? The issue is that to effectively serve children with special needs, schools need qualified teachers, comprehensive ongoing training for staff, knowledgeable supervision of teachers, non-classroom support services and in-class support for teachers. Much of those resources have never materialized, largely because federal funding has never come close to the 40 percent cost of paying for services to children identified as eligible for special education.

Further, given the lack of funding for proper services to children identified as needing special education, school districts rightly fear that once a child is identified, the school will be legally responsible for providing a quality education, when it is clear that in many cases they cannot deliver on that promise. This has led to the further problem of tremendous underidentification of children, in addition to the continuing practice of shipping children away from their homes and schools.

All too often, when services or supports do not exist in the community, officials tend to look elsewhere rather than develop the needed resources. They determine that the level of support cannot be created within the community. Ironically, the concept of "least restrictive environment" is commonly used in the opposite way it was intended, as a prescription to say the disability is too severe and thus "the least restrictive setting" is determined to be a treatment center out of a child's home community.

With so many districts claiming that they cannot afford to finance resources within the community for children with special needs, how can they possibly pay for the costly intensive inpatient facilities where so many of these children end up? While community-based care is almost always less expensive than out-of-home options, if a school district can show that the level of need is too high for a child to be served within the school, many states will pick up as much as three times the average per-pupil cost to pay for serving the child out of the district. In other words, there is a powerful financial incentive to label a child as having a severe disability and needing an out-of-community placement. The state becomes the funder of first resort, which "wipes clean" any community responsibility.

This strategy is appealing on more than a financial level: all too many teachers, schools, and districts would much prefer not to have to deal with children with serious disabilities in their classrooms and schools. Parents of children who do not have disabilities also often put pressure on schools to "remove the troublemakers."

While these problems persist today, thirty years after PL 94-142 passed, there are now many places where school districts, mental health agencies, and parents have worked together to create the kinds of community-based systems of care that are the focus of this book. However, they have been a long time coming. When the law passed, and for years afterward, the vast majority of children with serious emotional disturbance never received close to an appropriate level or quality of services; many more were shunted off to institutions that harmed more than helped them.

The backdrop had been set for Jane Knitzer to write her powerful book *Unclaimed Children* (1982), which shocked the nation by laying bare the desperate state of children and youth with serious emotional disturbance throughout our nation. Knitzer detailed a litany of ills: these children dropped out of school at an alarming rate, they had a higher than normal teen pregnancy rate, they were being sent in droves to out-of-state facilities with little oversight or real treatment, and they were receiving meager outpatient counseling when what they needed was a range of community-based services and supports. Knitzer's inescapable conclusion was that there was a national systems failure for children with mental health disabilities.

The National Institute of Mental Health responded to this dire problem with a small grant program begun in 1984, the Child and Adolescent Service System Program (CASSP). Each state was provided a modest amount of funding to develop a plan to address the mental health needs of children who were experiencing a serious emotional disturbance through a comprehensive, community-based approach. The funding was specifically aimed at *designing and planning* new approaches; money for services was not included. Crucial to this effort was the development of a set of guiding principles. Robert Friedman and Beth Stroul are credited with comprehensively describing these principles (1986).

System of Care Principles

Families as Partners

Systems of care require that families of children be involved in all aspects of the work. Whether designing or implementing a system, or evaluating or creating policy to support the system, family members need to be considered key partners with professionals. Treating families as partners means more than having token parent representation at meetings and on boards.

Families need to be provided with training and tools to be able to operate as equals in decision-making, on matters ranging from their own child's plan of care all the way up to state-level policy and practice matters. All meetings pertaining to your system of care need to have families sitting at the table. While this appears to many to be a revolutionary concept, once the concept of "families as partners" is truly embraced, this is the way mature systems of care operate as a matter of course. The now common cry of family members, "Nothing about us without us," says it all.

Interagency Collaboration

A key paradigm shift occurs within systems of care when all state and local child-serving agencies work together on behalf of the population being targeted. Interagency collaboration in the form of teams, committees, and governance structures should be part and parcel of the infrastructure. Many children involved with one agency, such as mental health, child welfare, education, or juvenile justice, end up needing services from a number of public agencies. Interagency teams need to be put in place to ensure that plans of care are individualized and address the whole child, and that all relevant agencies are bringing their resources to bear on each particular child and his or her family. State and local interagency teams are also able to resolve crosscutting issues around policy, program gaps, and funding. Further, only through interagency efforts can system-wide issues concerning management information systems, training programs, blended funding strategies, and unified communication plans be dealt with effectively.

Successful interagency collaboration means viewing children as a community-wide responsibility. This replaces the old paradigm whereby a child would be considered a "child welfare child" or a "mental health child," and agencies would try to push off a child with challenging and potentially costly needs to one another.

Individualized Care

At the heart of a system of care is the notion that each child and family is unique and has strengths, and that plans of care should focus on those strengths and individual qualities. The wraparound process and multisystemic therapy are two evidence-based interventions used within individualized plans of care for youth involved or at risk for involvement with mental health, child welfare, or juvenile justice systems. Other intervention strategies used in both mental health and child welfare include family group conferencing, family-focused therapy, family preservation, and family decision-making practice.

Individualizing care requires involving families and other natural supports. The plan of care needs to ensure that families' cultural considerations are addressed, that financial resources to support the plan are blended from all relevant public and private agencies, and that the plan calls for support of children within their home communities.

Cultural Competence

One of the most powerful principles that will determine the success or failure of a system of care is cultural competence. In order for plans of care to have meaning, relevance, and power for a child and his or her family, the plans must consider families' cultural backgrounds. For example, an Oglala Lakota tribal member's plan of care will need to respond to the healing traditions of the tribe. The same is true for all racial, ethnic, and cultural groups in this country. Agencies serving families need to ensure through policy that staffs receive cultural competence training and that the staff is culturally diverse and reflects the community where work is being done. Involving families in system-of-care planning increases the likelihood that it will be culturally competent.

Community-based Care

Children and youth thrive within the context of their homes and communities. The natural supports of family, friends, and institutions like schools, recreation centers, and places of religious worship are important stabilizing factors for children with special needs. Building systems of care within communities provides greater assurance that all the benefits of community life are extended to children and families receiving services and supports.

When children are removed from their communities to receive services, a number of negative factors come into play. For example, the peer group that the youth develops away from home creates a disincentive to return home. Youth placed out of their communities miss many of the age-appropriate markers that define growing up. Moving is a major stressor for anyone; by moving children outside their home communities, and thus cutting them off from their natural supports, an already difficult situation may be exacerbated.

Accountability

A hallmark of organized systems of care is the outcome data generated at the system and individual level. Interagency management information systems (MIS) can enable agencies to access data across agencies on behalf of the children being served. The information should track all the key demographic factors, number of children served, custody status, referral source, primary and secondary problems at intake, previous service history, family history, school performance, current living arrangements, caregiver strain, substance use history, costs, services and supports an individual receives, as well as duration and outcomes of those services and supports. (Center for Mental Health Services, 1998). Yet at the same time, the MIS must have stringent requirements to guarantee confidentiality, so that families and their children will be comfortable providing information about themselves and their histories.

System factors such as the extent of interagency collaboration, family involvement, blending of funds, cultural competence, policy development, levels of individualized care, and community-based care also should be gathered. This information about the process enables system leaders to determine to what extent they are truly operating under system-of-care principles, rather than just giving lip service to some of them. (Center for Mental Health Services, 1998).

WHY ARE THESE PRINCIPLES SO IMPORTANT TO SYSTEM CHANGE WORK?

First of all, no one child-serving agency can do everything for children. Only through *interagency collaborative relationships* with other child-serving agencies do we even have a chance. Creating that sense of interdependency also leverages the most money and diminishes the impact of any one department losing some of its resources because of a budget cut, grant loss, or new governor favoring one department over another. Another consideration is that legislatures are much more willing to fund new initiatives when all relevant agencies are working together. One quick way to exit the statehouse with a financial goose egg is to expose that the key players are unwilling to collaborate.

For too long we have settled for agencies working alone, with the result that children may have two or three care coordinators and several therapists, all from different agencies, while being told that another needed service is too expensive or nonexistent. If agencies did a better job of working together, the money saved from collaboration could probably buy those needed new services. We must be good businesspeople in human services. Our legislatures demand it, the children deserve it, and taxpayers need to see that their investments are effective and efficient if we expect them to invest more funds in our community systems. When you think of infrastructure, interagency collaboration needs to be at the front end of that thinking.

Since I've introduced the notion of business, let me move to the issue of *accountability*. Our history in human services has been that we serve people, we do not collect data. Early in our systems-of-care work we were able to garner federal and state financial support through parents sharing their compelling stories of what it was like to try to raise and support a child who has a mental health disorder. But over time, it has become clear that stories alone are insufficient. We need to back up those stories with data. We need to show the legislators, who are accountable to the voters, that investing in systems of care yields good results. It is incumbent on us to demonstrate that it makes a financial and clinical difference to support children in their own *homes and communities*. We all need to see this aspect of our work as critical to the long-term survival of systems of care.

In the Comprehensive Community Mental Health Services for Children and Their Families Program (the federal grant program supporting systems of care in communities and states across the country), we purposely included a strong evaluation component to show Congress and the administration that systems of care make a positive difference for children and families. The data backing up this claim have helped the program grow from the initial $4.9 million investment in 1992 to its current annual appropriation of well over a hundred million dollars.

Clearly, the most invested stakeholders in systems of care are the parents of children with mental health disorders. The parent voice is straight from the heart. It can ground everything from policy development and service priorities to what should be included in an individualized care plan. Parents are the real risktakers. They have nothing to lose and everything to gain by having a well-developed and successful system of care. When everything is mired in keeping the status quo from moving, it is almost always parents who can help dislodge the future from the past. Keep them in the mix at all times.

Plans succeed or fail depending on the integration of *cultural competence* into the effort. We are blessed as a nation to have one of the most, if not the most, diverse cultural and ethnic demographics of any country on earth. And yet, we have not celebrated that fact or embraced the many lessons of our rich diversity. Mental health has different meanings in different cultures. We must attend to these if individualized plans of care are to succeed. Our service providers need training in cultural competence, and agency policies must support culturally competent services and supports, including a range of culturally specific services for the individual child and family.

Systems of Care: From Planning to Reality

During the early months and years of the CASSP grant program, grantees were very supportive of one another and helped build a knowledge base for each to contribute to and expand. For example, one dedicated and creative professional from Ohio did a wonderful job of developing some of the first statewide interagency teams. A CASSP director from Pennsylvania was good at bringing funding streams together; a Pennsylvania parent was a savvy family leader and visited many states to help them begin the process of family involvement; a professional from South Carolina was further along in the area of cultural competence and shared his successes with the rest of us; and a North Carolina CASSP director who was particularly strong in public relations demonstrated some of those skills for the rest of us.

Soon after the CASSP system-of-care planning grant program started, the National Institute of Mental Health funded another new smaller program, the Family Network and Support Program. This three-year grant program began in 1987, offering $10,000 annual grants that, over time, have risen to their current level of $70,000 per grantee. The grants aim to help create and strengthen legitimate family organizations for families of children who have serious emotional disturbances. The family organizations offer parents and other family members significant support, providing information, sharing families' personal experiences advocating on behalf of their children to other families, and guaranteeing families a place at the policy table in states across the country. Out of those early grantees of this program rose a national family support and advocacy organization, the Federation of Families for Children's Mental Health.

The Child and Adolescent Service System Program ended in 1994. CASSP had served its purpose: to help states design their systems of care for children who were experiencing an emotional disturbance.

Now, beginning with the small appropriation in 1992, the Comprehensive Community Mental Health Services for Children and Their Families Program began, as a federal grant program to fund communities to start *building* community-based systems of care with funds to support services and infrastructure.

The baton was passed from strategic planning to service- and system-building.

In between CASSP and the new Children's Mental Health Services Initiative, from 1988 to 1992, was an important grant program funded by the Robert Wood Johnson (RWJ) Foundation. Its purpose was to test the concept of actually implementing the system-of-care principles in communities with groups of children and youth who had serious emotional disturbance, many of whom had been placed in out-of-home, and often out-of-state, facilities. Of the forty applicants, seven sites were chosen for the four-year grant program. Grantees were expected to blend dollars from all the child-serving agencies, to individualize a plan of care for each child served within the home and community, and to collect outcome data in order to determine whether children served in community-based systems were able to maintain their mental health.

The findings of the RWJ initiative were presented in a congressional briefing in 1992. The results showed that children and youth with profound mental health disorders could survive and thrive in communities that built a system of care and offered individualized plans of care, including significant clinical services and supports. The reporting of the results coincided with the growing advocacy to begin having the federal government fund systems of care.

Today over eighty communities have benefited from funds from this program, and thousands of children and their families have had the opportunity to receive a range of services and supports in the context of their homes, schools, and communities. System-of-care grants have been funded in nearly every state and on a number of Indian reservations. The system-of-care language and principles are gradually becoming infused into our understanding of how to most effectively serve children and youth with serious emotional disturbance in communities and states across the country.

Furthermore, a number of other federal agencies have adopted the system-of-care approach and are trying it with very different populations. System-of-care principles are benefiting youth with special health-care needs, various populations of youth in the child welfare system, youth in the juvenile justice system, children and youth who have traumatic brain injury and spinal cord injuries, and children and adolescents in Native American communities.

For example, in 2003, the federal Administration on Children and Families' Children's Bureau began a program called *Improving Child Welfare Outcomes through Systems of Care.* This program allows child welfare agencies to take the lead in designing their systems of care. The impetus for this new program was the results from the recently initiated federal Child and Family Service Reviews. Every state performed poorly, a clear indication that significant improvements in serving children in child welfare systems were long overdue. Despite the dismal situation highlighted by the reviews, one area of promise was that children did better in locations where systems of care were in place. Based on that finding and the close relationship that the Children's Bureau has with the Center for Mental Health Services and its system-of-care program, the idea was born to see whether target populations in the child welfare system could benefit from the system-of-care approach.

The future is bright for organized systems of care, with a few caveats. Keeping the integrity of the system-of-care model as it expands to populations beyond children with mental health disorders is critical. We must create strong evidence-based services within those systems of care and we need to devote considerable resources to helping communities develop confident, disciplined leadership to move from old service paradigms to new community-based system-of-care approaches.

A System of Care Story

The following real-life example illustrates the power of individualizing care, which is at the heart of a successful system of care. A young man we will call John had been sexually abused as a young boy and had an identified emotional disturbance and a substance abuse problem. One day in school he hit his teacher. This incident was his ticket to an out-of-state residential treatment placement, which is all too often the way such a situation is dealt with.

Soon after John was sent nearly a thousand miles away, his home state began reviewing the cases of children in out-of-state facilities. Interestingly, the investigation found little difference between profiles of children being served in-state compared with those served out-of-state, with one notable exception. The home communities of the children in the out-of-state facilities overwhelmingly claimed they lacked the clinical expertise to serve the children who ended up being placed out of state. At least they thought they did not have that ability. A bigger question was, did they even want to serve those children?

Many communities seem to take the attitude, "Let's remove this troubled child from our community. We will all be better off when he or she is gone." For others, it truly is a question of getting the technical assistance needed to strengthen their clinical skills in order to effectively serve young people with a serious emotional disturbance in their home communities.

Back to John. The team members who went out to meet John found out some interesting information when they focused on his strengths. They learned that he liked to cook, as well as write and draw. Here is the magic of individualized care and strength-based assessments! This is also an ideal opportunity to bring an individualized care team or wraparound team into the treatment mix. Creativity and innovation are the two most important tools of these teams.

The planning work now began to bring John back to his home community. Rather than place him back in his class full time, which he had departed suddenly and with negative feelings on both sides, the team, with John and his mother participating, decided that he would try working in a local college kitchen. Here he could use and further develop his cooking skills. At the same time, much of John's math requirements could be satisfied by his working with the accountant assigned to the kitchen. His English classes were tailored around writing his own cookbooks. The books also played a role in his art classes, as he drew the dishes that he created.

John spent part of the day in school, where there was an intensive-care coordinator who worked with the school, the college, his mom, a therapeutic foster care home where John temporarily resided, and his psychiatrist, to make sure the plan was synchronized and all parties were informed of progress and needed adjustments to the plan along the way. Within six months John returned to his mother's home. He continued to make progress in school, and his mental health vastly improved. He completed at least two cookbooks. It would not be fair to say that all has been smooth since then, but the bottom line is that John has been able to survive and even *thrive* in his own community. At one time, this was not seen as an option.

Establishing trusting partnerships among education, child welfare, and the local community mental health center was a crucial factor in John's success story. Unfortunately, it is hard to conceive of achieving this kind of major system change in many communities today. Yet it can and does happen.

Constructing your community's system change effort from the ground up, starting with relationship-building among the various stakeholder groups, is critical. But given all of the work such an effort entails, why would people and agencies bother to come together in the first place?

It is the tremendous caring about the welfare of children and families on the part of some key individuals that drives communities to want to join forces. Once that energy is marshaled and formalized through interagency processes and structures, the creative energy of people enables them to design services and plans of care that are unique, dynamic, and responsive to each child and family. There is nothing like a common task to spark that kind of bond among various agencies and stakeholders.

In the case of John's community, it was a shared desire by leaders from the local education system, the child welfare agency, and the community mental health center to build their community-based system of care that made the difference early on. Caring about the children in one's community is the common bond. The team structure creates the forum for an expression of how the common interest can yield new results.

There is another lesson here as well. The worst time to make decisions concerning his or her future is when a child is in crisis. A crisis plan needs to be activated, helping to stabilize the child. Not until the crisis subsides should we reevaluate the situation and put together the individualized care plan that responds to the particular needs and strengths of the child. How often do we do fail to wait, and instead remove children from their homes and communities in the midst of the crisis?

We know that having children stay in their homes and communities works. We know that the community environment allows for natural supports that have powerful positive influences on children, such as friends, neighbors, and organized religion, to be available, many at no cost. So why is it so hard to build that community-based system of care? Hundreds of years ago, Machiavelli provided a sage warning that stands to this day: do not underestimate the power of the status quo. Let me just list a few of those forces against change; note whether any of them resonate for you:

1. Longstanding contracts with out-of-state facilities by state, county, or city public agencies.

2. Negative stigma attached to having a mental health disorder or any disability.

3. Lack of public agencies collaborating on behalf of children (turf issues).

4. Lack of service array in the community. (This is interesting because the money to develop these services sits in all those contracts in out-of-state facilities—often millions of dollars!)

5. Financial disincentives to keep children in their communities.

6. Unwillingness on the part of service providers to do the clinical work differently (out of the office and in schools and homes).

Another brief but far-reaching quote from Machiavelli is, "Change has no constituency." Machiavelli suggested that the stake that the minority has in preserving their certain place in the status quo is far stronger than the stake the majority has in bringing about an uncertain alternative (O'Toole, 1995).

Another Story—Pacing Change

As the first director of children's mental health for Vermont some eighteen years ago, I was charged with leading the effort to implement the state's new system of care for children with serious emotional disturbance and their families. I thought it important to meet quite regularly with the children's directors of the ten community mental health centers in the state. Figuring it was an idea that made a lot of sense, I suggested at a monthly directors meeting that a number of parents of children with mental health disorders be allowed to attend so we could begin to better understand their needs and wants for the emerging system of care. Simple enough, right? Wrong! At that point, the thought of having parents at the meeting was too much for the directors. Some were still of the mindset that the parents were the reason that children had mental health disorders. Why would they want to hear from these "troubled" parents?

I quickly backed off, realizing that I had to bring a new level of understanding to them before they would embrace the concept of family involvement in systems of care. My plan had to change and the time span for this aspect of the work needed to stretch out. I decided to bring in some eloquent parent leaders from Vermont and elsewhere in the country to diminish the stereotypes of parents and replace the old view with new information. In time this adaptive challenge (a concept that is discussed at length in chapter 5) was met and we could move on in our system change work (Heifetz, 1994).

Reinforcing and Sustaining Systems of Care

The system-of-care principles described earlier have been my guide since I first began this work and have provided the framework for system-change efforts throughout the country. Our systems of care need to be: *culturally competent, home and community based, child and family focused,* and *strength based*; they must have *interagency collaboration* and *families as partners*; and the system of care needs to be *accountable*. These principles resonate as well today as when they were first introduced. They have stood the test of time, having been adopted and embraced by thousands of people across the country. You can never say them enough, and they continually need to be reinforced.

In order to ensure that the system-of-care concepts gain and maintain wide support, we need to confront an area that traditionally has lacked emphasis in our work: *public relations and social marketing*. I strongly recommend that communities embarking on system-building efforts develop a social marketing strategic plan. Pulling together a cross-systems team to focus on this issue is critical.

All the good data in the world are of no value unless you use them. Providing press releases and presentations to key stakeholders, creating newsletters, and finding radio, television, and newspaper opportunities are all key to building momentum for new systems of care and sustaining them.

I have seen public agencies undertaking new approaches take the attitude that the less publicity about them the better. This way they can operate "under the radar," with less chance that they will draw public criticism. That strategy has one major flaw: inevitably they do find themselves in the news, and it usually is for something unpleasant, if not downright alarming. If we build a relationship with the media that weaves in the positive results we are seeing, there is less likely to be a public relations nightmare when the occasional negative sound bite hits the papers and airwaves. We are in a competitive market economy, and if we are going to win the purse strings of legislatures and other funders, we need to capture the hearts and minds of the public regarding children's mental health and systems of care.

Finally, effective leadership and policy development are two intangibles crucial to successful system-of-care development and sustainability. Given the extent of change that will take place, leaders who understand and are schooled in system change are far more able to withstand the inevitable pressures and challenges. Creating administrative and legislative policies to sustain your system of care is vital to support-system stability in the face of changes in the economic and political climate.

STRATEGIC PLANNING

Frederick Law Olmsted, the designer of Central Park who is responsible for creating the field of landscape architecture in this country, said two things that ring so true to our work. These pearls of wisdom are quoted in *A Clearing in the Distance* (Rybczynski,1999). The first is a simple statement: "Before you build anything you must first design it." Now that seems to be common sense, but how many times are programs and services put together without much thought about how one service affects the other or the potential impact of a new initiative on the overall system? How often are we driven to add or subtract a resource based on money versus need? And how few times do we actually create and then follow a road map to get from here to there? Plan before you build. Think of creating the most beautiful building that you can imagine. Think of all the blueprints, site preparations, and planning steps that occur before one shovel of soil is lifted. Should we be any less vigilant in human services?

Olmsted's second statement is: "When we do build, build for our children's children's children." If you go to New York City's Central Park today, you will see trees that Olmsted planted some 150 years ago. Think of the changes around them that they have withstood! Our systems of care also must be strong and resilient, to withstand the inevitable political, economic, and social changes.

ARE WE READY FOR THE CHALLENGE?

Are you ready to build a system of care? Yes, it is the right thing to do for children, families, and communities. Yes, it will be difficult work. Finally, yes, we as a nation will be better off for your efforts. But are *you* ready?

This will be difficult work. Chances are very good that you will be maligned: painted as a traitor, undermined, gossiped about, yelled at, and betrayed. At times, children and their mental health needs will be the farthest thing from people's minds because all this change has them so riled up. Getting rid of you and bringing back the old days, before all the uncertainties and new tasks and different expectations, will be paramount for them. In order to persevere, you will need to be disciplined, always open to new learning, flexible, and ready for the inevitable unexpected twists and turns, both positive and negative.

Are you ready? I think you are if you fully understand the personal commitment and difficulties this undertaking will require. I think you are if you know in your heart the benefits this work will bring to children and families. I truly think you are if you are fully committed to the dream that one day soon all children, no matter what their disabilities or problems, will live together with their families in their home communities. What in life has real meaning that is not accompanied by risk and is not difficult?

REFERENCES

Center for Mental Health Services, (1998).
Evaluation of the comprehensive community mental health services for children and their families program, Orc/Macro International, Atlanta, GA.

Council for Exceptional Children Campaign,
Full Funding of IDEA newsletter June 2002

Heifetz, R.A. (1994).
Leadership without Easy Answers. Cambridge, MA: Harvard University Press.

Heifetz, R.A. & M. Linsky (2002).
Leadership on the Line. Cambridge, MA: Harvard University Press.
O'Toole, J. (1995).
Leading Change. San Francisco: Jossey-Bass.

Rybczynski, W. (1999).
A Clearing in the Distance. New York: Scribner.

Stroul, B. & R. Friedman (1986, revised edition, 1994)
Systems of care for children and adolescents with severe emotional disturbances.
Washington DC: Georgetown University Child Development Center.

CHAPTER TWO:

THE VERMONT EXPERIENCE—

A SYSTEM OF CARE CASE STUDY

Tell me and I'll forget;
show me and I may not remember.
Involve me and I'll understand.

—*Native American saying*

Introduction

Effective leaders know that honesty, dedication, creative thinking, political and business savvy, and undying respect for the power of a community of individuals to influence radical change are among the most vital characteristics of people who succeed in their efforts to make this world a better place.

This chapter will describe the role of leadership in mobilizing communities to carry out system reform from concept to implementation. It is important to note that my goal, through over three decades as a public entrepreneur, has always been to find better ways to engage stakeholders in a collaborative venture toward realizing comprehensive, coordinated, community-based, culturally responsive systems of care for all children and their families. With this in mind, you are invited to join me in an exploration of system change at the community level.

Like every other state in 1985, Vermont lacked an organized system that addressed the mental health needs of children within home and community-based settings. Stakeholders concerned about children had been crying for a more effective way to deliver services to children with serious emotional disturbances and their families. The agencies responsible (mental health, education, juvenile justice, substance abuse, child welfare, etc.) had until then existed and operated as discrete, insular entities, creating a loose patchwork of care fraught with inefficient gaps and overlaps.

Over the past twenty years, the state of Vermont has created its system of care for children with serious emotional disturbance by limiting bureaucratic inefficiencies, developing policies that promote home and community care, and building an interagency infrastructure that gives children and families the maximum access to a range of services and supports. Together these changes enable communities to assume a more central role in system reform, design, and operation.

In 1985, the then Department of Mental Health and Development Disabilities secured a five-year Child and Adolescent Service System Program strategic planning grant. As described in chapter 1, the purpose of the federal CASSP grants provided to each state was to design an integrated, cohesive system of care for children with serious emotional disturbance and their families. I was fortunate to have the position of Vermont CASSP director, overseeing the work funded through this planning grant.

BUILDING A SYSTEM OF CARE

In designing and implementing a system of care for children with serious emotional disturbance and their families, leaders must provide all stakeholders with a vision and sense of purpose. That vision was and is centered upon the system-of-care principles that shaped the entire process of reform:

- Families as partners in all aspects of the undertaking

- An interagency approach to address the needs of the children

- A focus on the child and family strengths rather than pathologies in building an individualized plan of care

- Cultural competence in constructing a system that is responsive to the unique needs of all people in a community, and

- The central notion of home- and community-based services underlying system design.

Establishing Infrastructure and Gaining Support from Key Stakeholders

In an effort to ensure that all stakeholders had a voice in whatever system of care we designed, I created a steering committee consisting of families, providers, political leaders, and state and local administrators across the child-service systems of juvenile justice, health, education, mental health, substance abuse, and child welfare. This committee incorporated a state-level legislative voice, with two House members and two Senate members. Schoenberg (1995) explains that once the leader has crystallized and extended his or her vision of core values and principles to the people, he or she must then create strong support among key stakeholders such as child-serving agencies, schools, families, and community members. From the inception of the steering committee, we realized the importance of including the Vermont community in open forums in each part of the state, with steering committee members to share local stories that demonstrated what they felt was needed to create an ideal system for children and families.

Kouzes (1987) notes that "by consulting with others and getting them to share information, leaders make certain that people feel involved in making decisions that affect them" and that "by seeking diverse inputs, leaders . . . provide a more open forum for competing viewpoints to be aired . . . enabl[ing] the leader to incorporate aspects of people's viewpoints into a project and demonstrate to others how their ideas have been heard and included." In an effort to open a public forum of information exchange with the communities, the steering committee met in each of Vermont's twelve catchment areas, which have essentially become the twelve community systems. The steering committee got together every other month, meeting in the off month in subcommittees, taking over two years to complete the tour of the state of Vermont.

The steering committee meetings always began with a public forum so that families and community representatives could express their needs and comment on the strengths and weaknesses of the current state of service to their children and families. It also allowed us to convey our intentions and educate communities about our goals. After the public forum, community members could stay and listen throughout the official meetings, in which we addressed issues such as arriving at a common definition of "serious emotional disturbance," drafting legislation to institutionalize the system of care, and creating interagency agreements or blended funding mechanisms.

FAMILIES FIRST

From the start, we placed immense importance on involving families and communities in developing policies. When early meetings with community mental health center children's directors were held, the idea of including families as equal players in designing services was broached. At first, the response was less than enthusiastic, as many believed that families were the problem for any child who walked through a clinician's doorway, rather than part of the solution. In order to legitimize the role of families, it was important to start to bring families from other states into meetings with children's directors of mental health, child welfare, district directors, and others. Schoenberg remarks upon the importance of "find[ing] family members who are willing to share their stories. Personalizing the impact that a failed system has on families can help the community better appreciate the need for a new and different system of care."

The first families that became steering committee members were those we had met in the public forums. The families came to speak about their children who were in out-of-state placements, were about to be sent out of state, had been thrown out of school, or were entering into custody in order to get services. Many of these parents eventually became a core group in the development of the Federation of Families for Children's Mental Health in Vermont. It was critical to have families represented at the table regardless of the type of meeting.

SMALL INCENTIVES GO A LONG WAY

Acknowledging the contributions of others seems to be a matter of human decency, and yet few leaders take the time to do so. Realizing that small incentives can influence loyalty and foster competence and trust, leaders should find creative ways to maximize their resources so that those resources touch every person involved with the system.

For example, in Vermont, the Child and Adolescent Service System Program grant made it possible to buy dinner for the steering committee, whose members came from all across the state, and to have meetings at bed-and-breakfasts so that the people could enjoy some rest and relaxation after working long hours together on often-difficult issues. Another example was the allocation of resources to the Federation of Families for Children's Mental Health to oversee a new respite care program based in the community mental health centers. This decision sent a clear message that the services that families wanted most would be attended to first, and that they would be led by family representatives. The level of commitment and participation was strong throughout the whole effort, as the committee members volunteered their time, often working until late in the evening, or staying over and going to work early the next day, sometimes a few hours away from their office. Family members rallied and supported one another throughout the state and donated countless hours to ensure the reform movement's success. People worked tirelessly because they were invested in a common vision.

Finding and Communicating Common Ground

Our steering committee meetings were also a place to develop an information exchange to generate local publicity and support for our work, as well as to involve the public in this statewide effort. From my experience as an elected official in Burlington, I knew that the success of an idea within a community depended on that idea being heard, changed, massaged, and ultimately owned by the community itself. Meeting in the twelve local communities rather than in Waterbury, where the state government human services offices are, provided an opportunity for the steering committee to listen to community voices, minimize personal nuances and maximize public wants, and develop their ideas in the real world rather than within their own perceptions of how a system should function. One of the most important tasks at hand in the initial stages of system reform is the identification of common ground.

Common Language Leads to Radical Change

Because there were many diverse stakeholders who participated in the system design, we needed to develop a common language to align the array of issues and parties and to foster a broad-based agreement on values. First, we focused on developing a common definition of serious emotional disturbance. The seven or eight definitions in use in Vermont and throughout the United States at the time reflected the absence of a common language and contributed to an inefficient patchwork of services in which children received service in one system while simultaneously being denied it in another.

A "definition subcommittee" worked for two years to formulate a precise definition across agencies that would be used as an operating standard. The committee discussed and considered many agency-specific positions challenging their attempt to arrive at a common definition. For instance, federal laws governing the operation of state departments, as well as the particular definitions of various state departments, hindered any easy resolution. The private and public sectors also had different definitions. The complicating effect of money, evidenced by the broad definitions of well-funded departments and more restrictive definitions of poorly funded departments, further added to the difficulties. Overcoming these challenges, we did arrive at a common definition and proceeded to have each department sign an agreement to use it in determining eligibility for service in Vermont's System of Care.

As a result, there were significant changes in many systems in Vermont. For example, the state Department of Education, which had used the federal definition of serious emotional disturbance in selecting children eligible for services in special education, now implemented our broader definition to expand eligibility to children with emotional disturbance who had previously been denied service. As a result, regular education and special education now began to work together.

LISTEN TO THE COMMUNITY

When communities heard about a planning grant, they were not enthusiastic about spending money on planning. People seemed more interested in immediate fixes such as an extra therapist or program. Their complaints of lack of service and three-month waiting lists that led to out-of-state placements would not be alleviated by the addition of a few therapists or programs, but could only be effectively addressed by rethinking and restructuring the entire system. I had to gain the trust of the communities in the notion that formulating a plan to change the entire method of supporting children and families in communities would make the greatest difference down the road, more so than merely adding therapists or programs today.

Kouzes (1987) explains that "leaders who build trusting relationships within their team are willing to consider alternative viewpoints and to make use of other people's expertise and abilities." By meeting with stakeholders individually to hear their hopes and dreams, and performing a needs assessment that involved families and parents as well as professionals, I built trust.

I also attempted to gain the people's trust over the long term by providing for some short-term needs. An example of this was seeking federal funding for respite care soon after the needs assessment showed that was the No. 1 service that families who had a child with a mental health disorder wanted. No such service existed then. We received a grant and began to fund respite care, which proved to be a valuable short-term accomplishment that helped people see that things were beginning to change for the better.

Assessing Community Needs

The needs assessment conducted out of our office proved immensely useful. Our assessment went out to hundreds of professionals from all fields and agencies throughout Vermont, as well as to parents and families. We ranked the needs identified in the responses and submitted the top one or two in a report to the commissioners of child welfare, education, and mental health. They took those prioritized service needs and began to build budget requests for the legislature that were in agreement with one another.

The needs assessment also provided an information base that helped direct our efforts over time. The legislature would address the No. 1 need first and move on to the next need the following year. For instance, Therapeutic intensive home-based services was the No. 1 need in one year, and when that need had been addressed and satisfied, we moved on to the second, therapeutic foster care. Schoenberg (1995) has noted the value of phasing in system development and incremental change, given the difficulty of implementing major changes all at once. By prioritizing our change management plan, we never overwhelmed the legislature by submitting dozens of proposals simultaneously.

Core Services

Ideally, leaders use findings from needs assessments and the good guidance of family-driven interagency teams to set an agenda for the development or enhancement of core services. Katz-Levy, Lourie, Stroul, and Zeigler-Dendy (1992) have enumerated seven core services that provide optimum care for children with serious emotional disturbance: crisis services, home-based services, case management, respite care, therapeutic foster care, transition services, and school-based services.

As noted above, our needs assessment identified respite care as the most urgent, and therefore we made it the service we would pursue first. The grant for respite care was contracted to the Federation of Families for Children's Mental Health to manage through community mental health centers. A respected family member headed the grant and was responsible for training respite workers throughout Vermont. In order to get all the communities involved, the money was distributed statewide. Although each community could serve only a few families at a time, this approach enlisted support from families and neighborhoods across every part of the state. This was preferable to having only a few communities receive all the money and thus being the only ones who would have information about respite's impact to use to advocate for general fund dollars after the grant money went away.

We also discovered a need to develop individualized wrap-around care, intensive family-based services, and therapeutic foster care. To test the efficacy of these services, we worked with one of the twelve catchment areas to build a model program of core services. We quickly realized that in order to effectively start up these services we would have to simultaneously invest in training and technical assistance that would infuse the kind of cultural change and new thinking required to implement them in a meaningful way. For example, previously in community mental health centers, the clinicians rarely visited families' homes, but in intensive family-based services, clinicians would need to go into the homes. This represented a significant adaptive challenge for these workers (Heifetz and Linsky, 2002). Therefore, they required substantial training and support to take on their new roles. This model program proliferated, and the program managers of intensive family-based services became their own support group, developing standards and forming a training cadre that developed a curriculum.

The providers of therapeutic foster care and respite care developed this same program of support. They held conferences for their peers on an ongoing basis, and ultimately created practice standards that were used across the state.

One of the major tasks was to facilitate the spread of a model program to other communities, which we accomplished through funding conferences and other technical assistance to replicate the model program. Training the trainers or leaders of programs increased that impact exponentially, so investments in such activities were a wise use of limited funds. In addition, as with the respite program development, whenever it seemed sensible we used grant funds to support staff who pursued other funds to enhance services-development activities. Once we opened the doors of the new system, children and families were eager to take advantage of the services. A key function once we began to infuse service dollars into the emerging system of care was to strike a balance between the infrastructure development responsibilities and the program implementation work.

Effective Strategies for Program Implementation

Good leaders are visionaries who can see both the forest and the trees. They are people who either possess the skills or know how to delegate responsibility to people with the skills required to hit the ground running during the initial phases of program implementation. Program implementation experts are quite talented at continually improving and monitoring the balanced operation of the system.

In moving on to the implementation stage of statewide system reform efforts in Vermont, I will briefly discuss a few aspects of program design and focus on momentum issues involving the media and legislation and the role of political will in keeping it together. In Vermont, much time was spent on these aspects of implementation. The work of these other individuals created the groundswell of leadership-building that is necessary to maintain momentum for the growing system of care.

Vermont Interagency Teams Influenced Systemwide Changes

In Vermont, interagency collaboration at the state and local levels was codified into law in 1988. Local interagency teams meet regularly and are composed of the directors of the local child-serving agencies [e.g., child welfare, education, community mental health, substance abuse, juvenile justice, and other community providers] and a parent(s) of a child(ren) with an emotional disturbance. Their objectives are to (1) develop coordinated services plans for children whose needs cannot be met by their individual treatment teams, (2) design new services in their region, and (3) bring unresolved problems regarding systems and individual treatment issues to the attention of the state interagency team. The state interagency team is composed of similar representatives from the state level offices as well as family members. This team addresses individual problems and suggests solutions. This hands-on case review allows state officials insight into needed reforms in the system. Teams at both levels work together to plan, implement, and more recently, govern new service delivery. (Schoenberg, 1995. p. 22).

State-of-the-art technologies were used to develop local interagency teams that worked together to find creative ways to help children and families get the resources they needed. We spent a great deal of time traveling around the state (outside the steering committee capacity) to bring people together. We would, for instance, allocate $3,000 to each community mental health center to forge their leadership role in the community, bring people to the table, reimburse parents for their time, have coffee and cookies, and enlist community support.

These interagency teams worked on individual cases as well as on larger scale system reform issues and strategic planning. Initially, local interagency teams were requested to bring to the table cases they had been unable to resolve for a theoretical discussion of possible ways to meet the children's needs. Eventually, they started to discuss real cases, and without our prompting, began solving those problems among themselves. It was in this very kind of loose exercise that the local interagency teams found their purpose.

The interagency teams learned that individuals in different departments were uninformed about each other's limitations imposed by law, and about the resources available to each department. As Heifetz states in a chapter titled "On a Razor's Edge" (1994), a leader "disorients people so that new role relationships develop; rather than quelling conflict, one generates it . . . challenging people . . . and raising conflict about direction." Similarly, we knew that the interagency teams would provide an opportunity for conflict to generate understanding. Typical conflicts included: child welfare workers criticizing mental health workers for not being present to meet children in their crises and merely engaging in an hour of therapy that ends once the child leaves the office; mental health workers attacking child welfare workers for being unwilling to engage a child unless he or she was in their custody; and other departments accusing the education department of restricting their definition of "serious emotional disturbance" in order to deny access to youngsters who did not fit the criteria of a child in need of services.

However, as the individuals from different departments began to collaborate on cases, they gained a better understanding of the limitations and responsibilities of other departments. For instance, the mental health worker realized that the child welfare worker was prevented by law from interacting and spending money on a child before he or she was in the welfare worker's custody. The child welfare worker also realized that the mental health department, through Medicaid, was able to provide a broader range of services than the child welfare department, but that given the child welfare law, had chosen not to deal with children in custody. The local community mental health center was limited by what it could provide for services by the contract it had with the Department of Mental Health.

Over time, a mutual understanding of the responsibilities and limitations of departments produced more collaboration and better coordination of services and benefits. As Kouzes (1987) explains, "Leaders must help to break down barriers between people by encouraging interactions across disciplines and between departments to produce collaboration which will ultimately improve performance."

System reform leaders bear significant responsibility in ensuring the public trust. Those spearheading interagency teams are particularly challenged by a multitude of issues and regulations that drive the day-to-day work of the interagency partners. Generally, interagency work should increase access to a broader array of services delivered in a consumer-friendly manner. The task of creating interagency teams to institute change required that we define specific goals and construct a path to achieving them.

One such goal was to increase access to services through the implementation of interagency teams at the state and local levels. In the first year of the grant, the Vermont Department of Education had identified some four hundred children as having a serious emotional disturbance. After modifying their definition of serious emotional disturbance by the fourth or fifth year of the grant, the figure increased to between eight hundred and nine hundred children. The department was willing to commit to serving these children because it believed that the cost of increasing access would be offset by the resources that could be provided beyond those of the education department. Another significant effect was the shift in perspective. Children were no longer locked into one department or another; they were no longer seen as "mental health" children or "child welfare" children or "education" children, but as "our" children, allowing the departments to share resources more effectively.

Goal two was to ensure privacy and confidentiality while simultaneously continuing information sharing between interagency teams. We had to persuade agencies to allow us to relinquish information on a particular child and family to other participants on these teams. The agencies agreed to this shift in policy provided that the parent agreed, and that the information would be made available only to those involved in formulating a treatment plan or some other systematic program for that individual child or family.

Goal three was to increase customer satisfaction by integrating and streamlining the system through interagency collaboration. Eighty-seven percent of the children passing through this interagency process had their needs addressed at the local level. The remaining 13 percent did go to the state level for resolution. The problems confronting the state interagency team effort concerned policy glitches, program gaps, and lack of money. For instance, by law, a child in state custody would be assigned to a child welfare caseworker, but if the child's problem was a mental health issue rather than a state custody issue, a mental health caseworker would obviously be more appropriate. As a result, the interagency team agreed to change policy at the state level so that the system could function more effectively in sharing responsibility to satisfy the true needs of the child.

Another example was that many of the plans of care that came in front of the state interagency team recommended intensive home-based family therapeutic services. Only one program of that kind existed when the state team first began operating. Within three years, armed with the information gleaned from the children brought to the state team's attention, each of the twelve catchment areas had a well-funded program supported by new general fund dollars matched with Medicaid.

Financial Management

Although the primary job of system administrators is to create and manage a budget for the services in their purview, even more important is that the leaders are skilled in maximizing resources to achieve a seamless, successful system of care. In addition, in this age of managed care and new ways of paying for and delivering services, leaders are faced with choices about setting rates for services that are accompanied by substantial risks. The consequences, pros and cons of choices such as case rates, capitation, and risk-sharing solutions must be studied carefully by leaders and stakeholders to protect the public trust and ensure that appropriate services are available for all children and families in need. Furthermore, poor choices in this regard can lead to the devolution of the provider infrastructure and hence the service system itself.

Successful system reform leaders begin seeking funds to sustain their systems the day they start up, not toward the end of the grant allocation. Creative leaders combine compelling stories of children and families with hard outcome data that demonstrate the worthwhile investment of funds to support children and families in need. Beyond making the case for an infusion of funds to adequately support the mental health needs of children and families, it is incumbent on system-of-care leaders to introduce evidence-based clinical practices that have been proven to support positive outcomes for recipients of those services. The combination of real-life stories, hard data, and proven interventions makes for a system that will produce continuing good results.

An outgrowth of the interagency team framework was the collaboration among the commissioners of education, child welfare, and mental health. The three commissioners as well as the secretary of human services were faithful in coming to biannual retreats to discuss the issues of the mental and emotional needs of children. As a result, the commissioners responded to the need for intensive family-based services, and collaborated to form coordinated budget proposals that were well-received by the legislature and resulted in funding such services across the state within three years. In the first year, the child welfare department received much of the money, thanks to the commissioner's relationships with the governor and House and Senate members, as well as his articulate and compassionate efforts. Eventually, the Department of Mental Health began to receive money, because it was using Medicaid. However, what's significant about these events is that rather than competing with one another for funding, the three commissioners collaborated and united on issues, thereby sending a powerful message to the legislature, which was then more willing to commit new resources. It really did not matter which department received the services money since all three departments were working so closely together.

We also found that our interagency teams produced case studies that influenced budget allocations across departments. For example, one of these teams presented a case of a twelve-year-old who had been sexually abused in her natural home, then repeatedly abused in a foster care placement. This young woman became suicidal while in a residential treatment placement with nine boys, gouging her eyes and cutting her arms. The local-level response to her situation was to send her case to the state interagency team, recommending an out-of-state placement. The state team was unwilling to send her to another facility after she had already been rejected by family and community. The state team approached the secretary of human services with a proposal to develop a treatment plan that would help stabilize her. The team separated her from the nine boys in the treatment center and then moved her into a small intensive therapeutic group home that had only two or three other children and was unique to her needs. The secretary provided the team with money to give to the local community to develop an intensive, twenty-four-hour treatment plan, seven days a week, which included medications and a very close intensive case manager, a school program, and other components.

We systematically collected and compiled information from cases like these, and the state interagency team would give the results to the commissioners of child welfare, mental health, education, and the secretary of human services at the biannual retreats. The information would assist the commissioners in developing budgets based on real-world experiences, triggering state-level reform based upon cases at the local level.

The Role of Communications in Maintaining Momentum and Sustaining the System

In system reform, leaders can be very helpful in setting the stage for engaging the media to inform the public as well as in garnering support and maintaining momentum for the new system. In Vermont, in addition to educating citizens about the mental health needs of children, the media also showed people the inadequacies of the state/local system.

Leaders need to be prepared to manage media inquiries and strategically seek media coverage of milestones in their movements' histories. For example, the public forums mentioned earlier were preceded by press releases describing the agenda and inviting the public to attend. Radio stations would often invite us for an interview before the meetings, or the stations would come to the public forums and broadcast the meetings on television. Community and regional newspapers often attended, too.

The Vermont CASSP office conveyed information from the state and federal level to local communities and vice versa. We used television and radio talk shows, and local and regional newspapers to circulate information about our emerging system of care. We held a press conference in the City Hall of Burlington (Vermont's largest city) when the three commissioners signed an agreement to develop the state interagency team. The media helped legitimize the system reform that was beginning to take place by reporting such events. This extra layer of support usually caught the attention of politicians, who closely monitor the media. As a result, politicians were generally well informed when approached with proposals. Press releases were also used to inform administrators and legislators about the results and progress of the system of care.

Schoenberg (1995) states that it is the responsibility of the leader to create incentives for staff to change to the new system by providing recognition and rewards for those who are able to move beyond their traditional roles in order to facilitate positive outcomes for children and families. Toward this end, we developed an interagency newsletter in Vermont (*New Directions*) for the professional and parent community to share information about new technologies, as well as to recognize good work. Every issue highlighted an individual who was making a positive contribution in the developing system of care. This type of public recognition served to validate and motivate team players in the new system of care. It was also an extremely effective vehicle for mentoring and role-modeling management and clinical leadership skills. The newsletter, which continues today, is also well-known as a forum for discussion of controversial issues.

Finally, in this era of managed care, it is essential that families and communities learn to articulate the values, principles, and success of the reforms they have crafted so that they are part of the good that will result from local managed care efforts rather than victims of the potential perils. A key to success here is learning to describe your reform movement in a marketable manner to multiple stakeholders, including those in the business community.

Communications consultants can be very supportive in helping analyze outcome and cost data and generating reports for print and broadcast media channels to further your cause of gaining the public's attention. The waves of rapid and unpredictable change that have accompanied the managed care movement in this country are only further evidence of the need to find ways to institutionalize those reforms that have been successful before the opportunity to do so is lost.

Culminating Momentum: Sustaining System Reform through Legislation

It is all too common that system reform efforts die shortly after the grant dollars that sparked their inception disappear.

It is the responsibility of leaders and communities to ensure that effective system reforms remain viable.

One way to accomplish this is to develop support from advocates who, through educational efforts, may be inspired to create regulatory support for maintaining the new system. Those who receive funds from federal sources are restricted from lobbying legislatures in any way. Leaders of federally supported movements must learn how to enlist advocates who will implement this part of the work when they feel the new system is worthy of their efforts. This kind of support is not usually hard to garner if leaders have taken care to include families and community leaders at all phases of the program design, implementation, and evaluation. Additionally, leaders may fund conferences and other educational forums to educate stakeholders on system accomplishments as well as advocacy skill building.

In Vermont, the momentum of community desire and information gathered from the state and national level coalesced in Act 264, which codified the body of system changes. A subcommittee of the steering committee was created to develop public policy, and the members decided to draft legislation to codify much of what we had developed through the CASSP grant program, such as local and state interagency teams, a unified definition of serious emotional disturbance, a governor-appointed system-of-care advisory board, a required yearly plan of action for the system of care and family involvement. A number of families were on this policy committee, and they added a section discussing the involvement of families in designing and implementing individualized treatment plans. The professionals would not have considered this idea, or the idea that the plan be developed after the child came in for a screening, had it not been for the family involvement.

In contrast to other laws that function as an overlay on a community's inaction, this law emerged and culminated from the momentum of changes and events that were already occurring. Because the reforms were already in progress, that momentum gave legitimacy to the law and kept the state moving forward toward approval. The legislators who were steering committee members missed many committee meetings early on, but were actually very effective in passing the law and overseeing future appropriations. With their help, the proposed statute was passed with minimal language modifications. Another factor facilitating passage was the absence of entitlements in the legislation, except for the entitlement to an individualized treatment plan. It was determined that the cost of entitling services to all children in Vermont with serious emotional disturbance would have been too much for any state legislature to deem acceptable. We believed we could progress year to year with the mechanisms we already had in place, thereby instituting a "de facto" entitlement, rather than a "de jure" entitlement.

KEEPING IT TOGETHER: MAINTAINING POLITICAL WILL

Conflict and controversy may undermine reform efforts unless the leader carefully manages them. It is important for a leader to endure and persevere through the challenging, questioning, and attacking that will inevitably arise with change. I have seen ideas foreign to politicians in one year being espoused by the very same politicians the next year. People require time to allow new ideas to sift through their minds before they begin to understand and appreciate them. *In Leadership without Easy Answers,* Heifetz (1994) refers to this type of phenomenon as a "ripening" in which conflict and confrontation are necessary for the development of an idea. System change is founded upon confrontation and the ability to handle it. Confrontation clarifies the vision. Unless a leader confronts and challenges the status quo, change is impossible.

As Heifetz and Linsky (2002) have stated, "exercising leadership from a position of authority in adaptive situations means going against the grain" They explain that "leadership is a razor's edge because one has to oversee a sustained period of social disequilibrium during which people confront the contradictions in their . . . communities." The leader must "raise conflict about direction."

In a similar vein, my job was to try and create a shared vision, to speak at the state and local levels about the direction Vermont was heading. At times when I would address the issues, direction, and mission, confrontations would emerge around individuals who were unwilling to change along with the reform. In one such situation, a community mental health center encouraged an individual to retire, and in another the agency reorganized itself and placed the individual in a position that was less directly involved in the collaborative work.

Leading a system reform effort often requires a changing of the guard. It is crucial for leaders to possess the ability to assess the strengths and potential of old staff, the fortitude to release those who need to move on, and the foresight to recognize and hire the right mix of new and successful team players.

It is important in system change that we not avoid confrontation (as many systems are apt to do, thereby becoming stagnant without momentum or leadership) but follow through with actions that some may perceive as painful at the time, ultimately with the best interests of the community in mind.

Staff Development: Considerations in Hiring

As the momentum behind the interagency system developed, a new breed of person was being hired: one who saw his or her mission as linked to the missions of individuals in other systems, an individual who viewed families as part of the solution and not part of the problem, and who perceived his or her role as a clinician being involved beyond the office, in the school, home, and community. The work environment was now extended to include the entire community. Because we redefined roles and goals of the system, we sought out staff with a skill and mindset different from those who worked in the old system. We would define the role, create standards for it, hire new people, and then meet with them monthly.

One example of nurturing service reform was to create a position of therapeutic case manager. The therapeutic case manager would be dealing with children who had in the past been sent out of state, and now were in their community. To work with these children, the managers needed the clinical knowledge and support, as well as a proper understanding of their new roles, to effectively care for the therapeutic needs of these children. To ensure access to the expertise needed, we hired a child psychiatrist to be their clinical supervisor. Providing monthly forums for open discussion among the therapeutic case managers was crucial to the ultimate success of this new clinical service.

The Provision of Training
and Technical Assistance

As noted earlier, it is the leadership team's responsibility to facilitate the spread of the system of care among local staff and other communities. In Vermont we accomplished this by funding conferences and using other forms of targeted technical assistance. An example was peer-to-peer matching. This approach allowed us to take what a professional, parent, program, or team had learned in a particular geographic region to another geographic region that could benefit from that particular piece of knowledge.

Investments in activities like "train the trainers" opportunities, state and regional conferences, and peer-to-peer technical assistance increased the likelihood of reaching a maximum number of people throughout the area. I also firmly believed in finding ways to foster creative thinking. Therefore I encouraged people to attend national or regional meetings, and to learn about new ideas generated in other places, as well as nationally accepted standards of practices. I have also found that bringing in national and regional experts to consult with site personnel not only provides needed guidance, but also creates incentive for local stakeholders because they tend to view this consultation as a gift. Training and technical assistance only work if they occur regularly. Building a yearly training calendar ensures that emerging training needs can be met in a methodical way.

Making Evaluation Happen

Performance-based contracting and report cards for service delivery performance have become mandates of federal, state, and local government entities. Thanks to technological advances, businesses thrive on information such as daily and hourly productivity reports. Responsible leaders in this day and age must carefully select the methods by which they will measure the effectiveness of their efforts at both the management level and the individual client level. It is equally important to know whether the reform movement made the community stronger and whether it influenced providers to deliver services that actually helped children and families find ways to function more productively and in a developmentally appropriate manner.

Leaders now know that their constituents will demand that they cycle back information and data about system performance to the community and that this is a crucial aspect of maintaining support and enthusiasm for their efforts. Data also serve to assist program officials in deciding upon the future path and next steps of the system.

In Vermont we established a relationship with the University of Vermont to work collaboratively on studies they already had under way as well as to commission outcome studies that would let us give the community the feedback it anticipated. From the outset, we emphasized that we valued evaluation by conducting extensive needs assessments, and we validated those assessments by funding new services in the order of the community demands we discovered through the process.

Later when we acquired a Robert Wood Johnson Foundation grant, which was a system-of-care service implementation initiative, we performed studies on the cost of implementing an individualized treatment plan for children, which was a part of the therapeutic case management wraparound system. Many services that were called for in the treatment plan were, in the end, not needed, and after three months, actual costs began to go down as the children improved. We also analyzed the cost of sending a child to an out-of-state placement, which was shown to be more expensive than the cost of developing individualized plans of care in the home community. These studies demonstrated that in wrapping services around a child in his or her home community, we could get good results for less money.

Our data analyses also showed that our individualized care system, if offered to all children who needed that level of support, would require substantial up-front investments, but that the ultimate cost per child would be lower. For instance, a child in foster care with unaddressed mental health needs would require more money to address those needs. At the same time, avoiding an out-of-state placement would save money, as these children who were being over served or served in inappropriate, high-end, expensive, out-of-state placements would be incorporated into the local system of care receiving individualized services. In addition, our data showed that the outcomes for these children being served in their communities were much better than if they were being served in a distant placement where the clinical gains could not be transferred to the home and family.

We also had a close relationship with the late Dr. John Burchard at the University of Vermont. Burchard was performing studies of children in residential treatment and children in community, analyzing success indicators for children, such as school attendance, grades, crime rates, and other factors that would increase for children in communities when they returned from residential treatment but would then taper down. We studied the contrast between children who returned from the isolated residential treatment center to the open community, and children who had treatment services wrapped around them in their communities. The differences between the two were significant.

Later as the federal branch chief and person responsible for overseeing the Community Mental Health Services for Children and Their Families Program, I worked closely with evaluators who orchestrated on our behalf the largest comparative outcome study in the history of child mental health service delivery. There have been many lessons learned from this effort and many incredible success stories. Among the most valuable lessons for me has been how important it is to build relationships with researchers and communications experts who can help you share stories about the data with your diverse constituencies in ways that are palatable, powerful, and honest. Equally important has been the involvement of multiple stakeholders in the evaluation, design, and implementation of evaluation itself. Multiple perspectives have enriched the evaluation and shed new light on the findings. Allowing time for this level of inclusion is not always easy, but it pays dividends when all parties are confident that the data truly represent the outcomes and are useful in the next phase of system development.

Conclusion: Retrospective View of System Reform and Implementation

This discussion has progressed through the stages of system development leading to the implementation of a system of care, using my experience in Vermont as a case in point. Ultimately, the responsibility of the state leadership is to support communities in building systems of care for children with disabilities and their families. A hundred years ago, the state's solution for people with special needs was to create a community outside natural communities. In the end they found they couldn't create a sense of community with large institutions: what people truly need are their neighbors, the sense of belonging to a community, the sense that they can contribute to community life regardless of the extent of disability. That fabric of community is very powerful, and costs not a penny, though it is priceless in its relationship to children with special needs.

The responsibility lies not only with the community, which is a subdivision of the state, but also with the state.

States must give communities the policies, services, and supports necessary to provide an effective system of care. This is the beginning and the end of the state's responsibility to the community. State officials err when, for political reasons, they refuse to support at the policy level innovative ideas that communities have formulated. A state's refusal to consider such ideas prevents communities from flourishing. The ideal situation is when the community enlightens the state while state-level leaders ensure support for ideas and systems most helpful to the people. It is important for state leaders to realize that solutions to many problems are actually present and embedded within communities. If state officials go beyond their offices into the communities, they will find answers to almost every problem.

America today has isolated community pockets of excellent public policy, services, and support to children with disabilities and their families. The challenge in this still new century is how to knit these pockets together, strongly and deeply enough so that all of America's children with special needs, and their families, can grow and flourish.

REFERENCES

Covey, S. (1992).
Principle-Centered Leadership. New York: Simon & Schuster.

Clinton, H.R. (1996).
It Takes a Village and Other Lessons Children Teach Us. New York: Simon & Schuster.

Fulghum, R. (1993).
All I Really Need to Know I Learned in Kindergarten. New York: Ivy Books.

Heifetz, R.A. (1994).
Leadership without Easy Answers. Cambridge, MA: Harvard University Press.

Heifetz, R.A. & M. Linsky (2002).
Leadership on the Line. Cambridge, MA: Harvard University Press.

Katz-Leavy, J.W., I.S. Lourie, B.A. Stroul & C. Zeigler-Dendy(1992).
Individualized Services in a System of Care (monograph). Washington DC: CASSP
Technical Assistance Center, Georgetown University.

Kouzes, J.M. (1987).
The Leadership Challenge: How to Get Extraordinary Things Done in Organizations.
San Francisco: Jossey-Bass.

Schoenberg, S. (1995).
*Making it happen: A guide to program development for services to children and
adolescents who are experiencing a severe emotional disturbance and their families*.
Washington DC: National Resource Network for Child and Family Mental
Health Services.

A similar version of this chapter appeared in Greenwood Press,
Where Children Live: Solutions for Serving Young Children and Their Families
(1999). Chapter 7.

CHAPTER THREE:

THE
NAVAJO STORY

*Leadership is practiced
not so much in words
as in attitude and in action.*

—Harold Green

INTRODUCTION

One of the major principles underlying systems of care is the need for services and systems to be culturally competent. Each ethnic group, race, and culture defines and responds to mental health disorders differently. The kinds of services, where they should be, the training necessary for staff to understand and appreciate a community's various cultures, and policies to reinforce cultural competence are all important. This principle has rarely been actualized in ways that would permit one to say, "This is a culturally competent system of care." In the national evaluation of the federal Center for Mental Health Services system-of-care grants program that I led, a "system-ness" measure assesses how communities are faring in realizing the values and principles of systems of care (family centered, interagency collaboration, community based, child-centered services, cultural competence, and accountability). Cultural competence has been consistently at the bottom of the list in terms of implementation levels within the grant communities.

It is from this cultural competence frame that the Navajo Story was written. A similar story could and needs to be written about African-Americans, Asian-Americans, Latino-Americans, along with other distinct races and cultures within the United States. This particular example dramatically illustrates how unique a people can be in how they live their lives, respond to mental health crisis, and define what is important about their lives in community. Whether the cultural distinctions are clearly visible or very subtle, they do exist for each culture, race, and ethnic group. My hope is that this chapter can help make the reader more willing to find those unique features within groups and tailor services and supports to meet those cultural anchors. Culturally competent services and supports can be the most powerful clinical interventions in the healing processes of individuals. There is no substitute.

A Place Called Community

During the course of the five years that the Navajo Nation had a grant with the branch, I visited twice. Both occasions provided an incredible opportunity to begin to understand the depth of the Navajo people: their culture, their land, and their spirit to move forward in the face of so much undeserved pain.

Early one morning, the site visit team (The federal project officer from my office in charge of this grant, her son, and I) assembled with approximately thirty people in a large hogan. The hogan, the traditional home of the Navajo, plays a significant role in the people's spiritual life. It was an exceptionally cold morning; the wind was still, and the comforting smell of the smoke from the nearby homes wafted over our small group. This was a big morning. We were going to meet with many of the community elders and several medicine men. What we federal folks did not realize was that the community had learned of the recent death of the project officer's husband and was preparing to offer a ceremony on her behalf.

The ceremony began with traditional prayers. The air was thick with healing powers that seemed to grip all of us—especially my grieving staff member and her son. Time felt suspended. As we went around the circle, each word spoken built upon the last to form a protective blanket over us all. Several hours had passed by the time we emerged from the hogan, but it could have been a few minutes or an entire day. Participating in this timeless tradition was a powerful way to begin our morning.

Later that morning, the director of the K'e Project drove us to a remote community in a trip that took hours. The landscape changed from small trees and brush to open red plains that were absent any sign of human intervention. The long ride across this uniquely lovely landscape, coupled with the morning's profound ceremony, had a great impact on me. I found myself musing on those vast "meaning of life" questions that rarely cross one's mind in the day-to-day frantic pace of life in Washington.

Our guide, the grant project director, knew exactly where she was going in this enormous open space. She made a right turn here, and a left turn there, on seemingly endless roads. The journey ended abruptly some three hours later at the side of another hogan. This structure was much smaller than the first but gave off the same feeling of deep spirituality; it was like walking into someone's private house of worship. We were visiting this home as a way to better understand the unique cultural underpinnings of family life in the Navajo Nation.

Inside the hogan, we were met by the grandmother, her granddaughter, and the granddaughter's child. The grandmother was somewhere between eighty and one hundred years old. She spoke only Navajo, so we communicated through an interpreter. I offered my appreciation for her inviting us to her home. The mother, who was not at the gathering, was not able to care for her daughter and child and so grandmother was helping. Kinship care exists in all corners of our country.

A member of our party asked the grandmother to show us how she worked the large loom by her side. At this point the most amazing transformation occurred. Immediately I saw a twinkle in the grandmother's eyes. Then it appeared as if she had changed into a body some sixty years younger than her own. She moved into position to work the loom with no wasted motion and incredible grace. Her fingers took over, moving across that loom as an accomplished pianist would move across a keyboard. She was making a most beautiful Navajo rug. This was her income, how she kept the family together and sustained them.

I left that home filled with thoughts about what is great about America—our rich cultural diversity; so many talented people willing to share their creations. But I was also left with a great sadness. I knew that while this family lives in poverty, a non-Navajo entrepreneur would buy that rug for a pittance and sell it for hundreds of dollars in profit just down the road in Gallup. There must be a better way; although to this day the solution evades me.

After leaving this family, our two-car caravan moved on to our next activity for the day: a barbecue/picnic to welcome us visitors. We stopped just outside Canyon de Chelly, Arizona, the spiritual center of the Navajo Nation. At least fifty people arrived: children, parents, grandparents, and the various staff doing the grant work. The food was spectacular, the traditional Navajo clothing was beautiful, and the carefree joy of the children was heartwarming. But most moving was the dancing we all did after dinner. We formed a large circle and proceeded to dance in that circle, led by Navajo voices and drums. We danced 'til the sun set. It was the Navajo way of welcoming us to their Nation.

Our next day began with a sunrise ceremony at the top of the canyon looking directly at Spider Rock, which, for the Navajo people, is the spiritual epicenter of their Nation. The air was fresh, the sun was glorious, and the ceremony lifted the spirits of all who were there. To see the significance of the moment and the insignificance of any one life by itself yielding to the power of the Creator that is within us all was so moving and uplifting. From the morning ceremony we visited a tribal community college, a local grammar school, and the regional social services office. We then headed back to the starting point of our trip. By that afternoon we were leaving Navajo country, heading south to a grantee meeting in Las Cruces, New Mexico.

If I needed something to snap me out of the intense experience I had just been part of, the next morning in Albuquerque, New Mexico, did the trick. The previous evening, we had driven to a hotel in Albuquerque. The next morning we packed our belongings, put them in the van and headed off to breakfast. The plan was to travel the five hours south to Las Cruces. While we were eating breakfast, someone rushed in to tell us that our van had been broken into. We ran out to the parking lot, where it was clear that our van's back window had been broken and most of the luggage had been taken. The most heartbreaking part of this event was that my staff person, who had just lost her husband, had pictures of the two of them in her luggage. The pictures were gone. So also were all my clothes, but they were replaceable. What was life telling us?

A Culturally Competent Response to Crisis

It was toward the end of another day on my second visit when I was asked if I would like to attend a ceremony being held in the home of a family where one son had just attempted suicide. I felt honored by the invitation and joined them.

Along with the medicine man, family and friends gathered in the house, and a small fire was lit in the center of the open living room. The young man was in attendance and looked to be in a somber mood. The fifty or so other members of the gathering all appeared to have heavy hearts. After some prayers by the tribe's medicine man, each member of the gathering was asked to speak. Every member of the group that night spoke from the heart. Each told a story of how he or she got to know the young man, his special attributes, and how terrible it would be if he was not there. Each story closed with a big hug for him from the speaker. The medicine man was the last to speak, and he summed up all the feelings of love and support for the young man.

As an outsider, and one who is concerned about the mental health of our young people, I was most impressed with the power of love that night. I can't tell you how the young man is doing today, but I can say that he knew that he was a part of a community, that the community cared about him, and that what he did, would have an impact. He knew that he was not alone.

The traditions of the ceremony call for the family to honor the medicine man with a thank-you gift for his role in the family's life and the community. This is always a significant gift that takes considerable time and work to accumulate and requires sacrifice for the family to pull together. The evening at that house somewhere in the Navajo Reservation impressed me deeply regarding what community is and the power that community can play in its members' lives.

In comparison, when I muse on mainstream American culture, I see how underdeveloped we are at using our natural communities. How seldom we come together to honor our youth and let them know how much we love them. We seem to be able to marshal our resources to send young people with problems to a therapist to "be fixed," rather than pull together all those who care about that young person and let the adolescent who is troubled know how valuable he or she is to the family and community. If Americans can make the effort to listen to and learn from our Native American brothers and sisters, we will become a richer nation for ourselves and for the world.

Exploring Cultural Differences

The project director of the Navajo grant, like so many of her counterparts around the country, was struggling with the impact the system change generated by the grant program was having on her community. Those who may have supported the change in theory were now confronted by the reality and did not necessarily want it. The tension this created, coupled with her own medical problems, had brought the project director to the point of examining what she needed to do for herself. She called and asked if I could join her for a few days and help sort out her next steps. She decided the best place to meet was in Canyon de Chelly. She allowed time for us to talk things through, but also invited many of her staff to attend. It would be a chance for me to talk to her staff about the importance of their work and listen to them about what the system of care that they were creating meant to them. We would all camp out next to a large stream near one of the staff's mother's home.

A project staffer picked me up at the airport in Gallup, and we drove a few hours to a spot at the edge of the canyon that was said to have a path leading down to the campsite at the bottom. I got out of the car thinking this would be a great adventure, fully expecting some steps and guard rails leading down the canyon. What I got was the director and her friend pointing to the "path." What I saw as I began inching my way down on my hands and knees was sheer rock that looked like it went straight down! As hard as I tried to move forward on that "path," I was paralyzed by the thought of falling. After about ten minutes, I gave up and said, "I have to find another way down into the canyon, this will not work!"

Most members of the party headed right off the boulders and on down the "trail." For me, they brought back the jeep. We went to the mouth of the canyon and drove some five miles upstream to the campsite. I didn't realize until later, though, that the stream was full of quicksand. My driver knew exactly where all the soft spots were and was able to avoid every one. He did show me in the streambed the roof of another jeep that was not as lucky! By the time we got to camp, there were the other party members arriving from "the path." To my amazement, they all made it alive and well.

Along the way, my driver mentioned that on the lands next to the stream, before the great massacre of Navajo in Canyon de Chelly by the US Army (more on this later), there used to be groves of fruit trees that would feed the people in the surrounding area. Those groves have never been replanted. I wondered aloud to the project director, "Wouldn't it be a wonderful cross-cultural exchange to have some youth come from urban centers to learn the Navajo ways and at the same time replant all those fruit trees? Similarly, some Navajo children could visit a large city, learn about a particular ethnic culture, and contribute to the community with an equally meaningful project." The Navajo project director also loved the idea, but because she soon left her position it never was actualized.

The project director and I went off to talk about her situation while others put the camp together. Given time and thought, the answer to what one does in the future becomes clear. My role was to provide some questions and be a willing ear for the project director's thoughts. She had put so much of her life into the work and had achieved amazing strides for her community. Now she was a bit worn by the experience and concerned about her health. She knew it was time to move on and take care of herself in the process. The system-change work that is a large part of building a community-based system of care for children who have mental health needs can be very difficult for the leader and the community. It often involves upheaval, deep conflict, and the loss of old alliances. Many of the leaders reach the point of wanting to leave within just a few years. Individuals who take on the job of system change need to be schooled in the finer points of leading during times of change. Training can help them learn to anticipate the inevitable resistance that generally accompanies significant change efforts and thus be able to better respond.

A Natural Leader in the Navajo Community

Back at the camp, the structures were up and the food was being prepared. Tents, a sweat lodge, and the fire made up the major portion of our little village by the stream. All of the men, including me, went into the sweat lodge and proceeded to help heal our various wounds of the spiritual kind. It was very powerful, and I was so honored to be a part of this incredible cultural experience. Now the sun was setting and dinner was to be served. Many of the vegetables were from the piece of land tilled by the director's friend's mother. We sat around the fire for some time, and then I noticed a vehicle pull up. The son of the project director's friend was driving, and he reported that a jeep was sinking in the stream. The driver in trouble was someone coming to camp from another tribe and was not familiar with the "soft" spots of the stream.

Everyone jumped into their vehicles and followed the young man down to the site of the sinking jeep, maybe two miles from camp. What we saw was stunning. The vehicle was lurching on its side with water running through the floorboards. It looked hopeless, at least from my point of view.

The young man who led us to the site immediately pulled out some very thick rope and attached his vehicle to the jeep in trouble. He got some planks of wood and set them under one wheel. The rest of us pulled up our pants and waded into the stream.

I must say it was the perfect night. There was a full moon, it was cloudless, and the temperature must have been around seventy degrees. If it wasn't for the trouble the jeep was in, I would have said this was just about as close as I have been to "heaven on earth."

Ever so slowly the men pushed the sinking vehicle while the young man's jeep pulled the rope tight. Wheel by wheel we were able to right the jeep until it was sitting evenly in the water. At one point while we were all pushing and pulling there was a funny interlude. Someone up front said, "Can the white guy bring up the flashlight?" I realized he was talking to me, as I was the only non-Native American person in the group! We all laughed and then went back to the task at hand.

After about two hours of hard labor and constant shifting of the boards under the wheels and the undaunted determination and guidance of that young man, we were able to bring the vehicle out of the water and onto a sandbar. I could not believe it. What amazing teamwork, what amazing determination.

Afterward, while reflecting on this event, I learned an important lesson from some of the men about why we all do this work in children's mental health. One person said, "This is what community is all about. There never was a question of, would we accomplish this task, it just had to be done and we would do it." I felt like I had walked into the heart of community. The work we did together that night defined without words what community is all about. Crisis brought opportunity to show just how much community existed there in Canyon de Chelly in the Navajo country.

The young man who led us in the rescue of the jeep was obviously very bright. I came to find out, though, that he had just told his mother he did not want to finish his high school degree. She was heartbroken. She knew, as others did, that he was an exceptionally intelligent young man, but his mind was made up.

As it turned out, the next day he offered to take me further up the canyon to see the beauty that only a few people had ever seen. What I didn't realize was that he was about to give me an unexpected history lesson. We hopped into the jeep and off we drove. He told me of the pain of his people dating back to when the US Cavalry came up the canyon and slaughtered hundreds of Navajo men, women, and children in their attempt to move them out of where we were driving that day. He spoke as if the events of that time had just happened. The wounds were very fresh and clearly had not healed. This young person had such a sense of himself. The more I watched and listened to him, the more I realized that he had such command over himself that whatever path he took would be the one he needed to take at that time.

We viewed homes and villages carved out of the cliffs that framed this canyon some two and three hundred feet above the ground. Although abandoned for years, they seemed still in waiting for their ancestors to come back. The secrets of the canyon were many, some hidden behind bushes, others carried on by oral traditions, but, unmistakably, the most powerful secret—which is really no secret—is that these were and are the holy lands of a proud people. I felt as if I had been escorted by an heir apparent to all of this, the next generation of proud and spiritually powerful Navajos.

When we got back to camp, I thanked the young man and told him how special my day with him was. I also told him that he needed to continue to use his own thoughts to guide his future. I soon found his mother and told her my belief that she had nothing to worry about, her son was an incredible young man who would make good choices in his life if given the opportunity.

Later that year the young man's mother wrote a letter telling me that he had returned to school, received his high school diploma, and decided to go on to college to become a physician. I was not at all surprised. Like him, the Navajo people are steeped in spiritual life, keenly aware of their place in history, and grounded in the realities of their current existence. Despite the many hardships they face, they are filled with pride, courage, and hope for the future.

This story is rooted in the notion that community is an essential part of culture. For the Navajo Nation, community is everything, whether it is to help a young man who had given up on life, to rescue someone in distress, or to share in the grief of a visitor. It is all done by the community coming together. If our systems of care are going to be successful across America, they will have to attend to the issues of cultural competence. This means delving deeply into the language, practices, and nuances of what each cultural group needs to help it define community. If we are successful, we

CHAPTER FOUR:

PARENT/
PROFESSIONAL
PARTNERSHIPS—

A CRITICAL ANALYSIS

*The biggest disease today
is not leprosy or tuberculosis, but
rather the feeling of being unwanted.*

—Mother Teresa

INTRODUCTION

Perhaps the most promising development in children's mental health and community-based systems of care in the last twenty years has been the gradual but ever-increasing family involvement. This involvement has meant change at every level, from how individualized care plans are developed for children and their families, to major policy shifts regarding how communities, states, and the federal government address the mental health needs of children and their families.

The change for both parents and professionals has been profound. Each group has had to adapt to the changing landscape in order to build working partnerships and keep them moving forward. This chapter attempts to capture areas of common ground as well as some of the tension points of this important partnership, and offers some solutions to overcome the challenges stemming from the differing perspectives of families and professionals.

A few years ago, while visiting a community in the process of building its system of care for children experiencing a serious emotional disturbance, I met with about twenty newly hired care coordinators. At one time, most of them worked in residential treatment centers; now they were employed by a community-based organization that was responsible for creating and implementing individualized care plans for children returning from residential treatment. What was astounding about these young professionals was that, almost to a person, they recalled that when they had worked in residential treatment centers they had seen it as a bother, almost an intrusion, when parents wanted to be involved with their child. It was as if the family got in the way of the professional's desire to work with the child without interference.

Now, in their new lives as community care coordinators, these same individuals unanimously placed a high value on having parents involved in treatment planning. In fact, they all talked about how impossible it would be to do their job if the parents were not part of the process! In their eyes, the role of parents had transformed dramatically, from being viewed primarily as a burden to being considered valuable members of the treatment team, with insight and unending energy and support for their children.

This changing perspective is having a tremendous impact on how both professionals and parents define the role of parents and family-led organizations in system-of-care development. We will take a look at the ramifications for professionals and parents as they work to create effective partnerships within systems of care. Ultimately, in order for a community to build a system that supports all of its children, rejecting none, all parties involved must undergo shifts in perception and changes in behavior. This dynamic is present whether this work is going on at the national, state, county, city, or community level.

The Beginnings of Professional/ Parent Partnerships

In 1987, a modest new federal grant program called the Family Network and Support Program was initiated by the Child, Adolescent and Family Branch of the National Institute of Mental Health (now the federal Center for Mental Health Services). Approximately ten grants of $5,000 per year for three years were awarded the first year, with the goal of supporting the start-up of statewide family support organizations. The competitive grant program has been renewed every three years, and has substantially expanded. The most recent grant competition, awarded in 2002, were for $60,000 per year ($70,000 if the organization planned to add a youth organizing component), with forty-one state organizations and one US territory receiving grant funding.

While $60,000 per year may at first appear to be a windfall, when yearly expenses are added up, it becomes clear that the federal funds provide statewide family organizations with just about enough money for office rent, supplies, phones, and a computer, plus a small amount to support staff. But it is a start, and provides a formal point of contact that helps professionals in various public agencies start building relationships with an officially recognized family organization. Families have been dealing with professionals for many years on behalf of their children, but usually in their roles as parents of children with special needs, requesting help from those in roles of authority, including clinicians, teachers, educational administrators, and the like. Building up family organizations has enabled a new form of interaction to take place, with parents approaching professionals in something resembling a relationship among equals, each of whom has valuable skills and knowledge to share.

In state after state, mental health and other agencies are at long last realizing the value of including parent organizations as partners in the network supporting children with serious emotional disturbance and their families. Many state children's mental health directors truly want to see their state's family organization become successful, and they arrange to contract with the organization for specific tasks and responsibilities related to family support. This is an expression of genuine interest in strengthening families' role and influence, and yet this new connection, especially the direct financial support from states, unfortunately often plants seeds of struggle.

Growing Pains: The Clash of Expectations Versus Reality

Most often, public mental health agencies provide funding to family organizations through a contracting mechanism. These are official contracts of the kind that states are accustomed to, with scope of work, specific tasks and timelines spelled out. This kind of formal agreement is often a first for a new family organization that in many cases has been a grassroots, volunteer group with almost no money, paid staff, lines of authority, written work plans, regulations, or other components of an established organization.

With a state contract, infrastructure and accounting procedures need to be put into place, and quickly. A set of skills is required that the new family organization may only partially possess, including writing, interviewing, budgeting, product development, and monitoring/evaluation. Handling the significant new organizational demands may be absolutely overwhelming to the new executive director, whose previous experience has been primarily handling those nonstop calls to the toll-free number and providing individual support to family members in crisis.

So much happens at once with a new family organization's growth through the infusion of the first significant funds. On the one hand, the parent leader is grateful to receive money that will help her organization grow, yet she now faces a whole new set of worries about all the accompanying rules and regulations. The parent leader may seriously doubt whether she has the skills to do a good job in her expanded organization.

The professional responsible for the contracting relationship also faces a multitude of issues with the new partnership. The first thought is likely to be one of great satisfaction in providing some state money to the fledgling family organization, along with the anticipation of developing a closer working relationship with parents who truly understand what children need.

Unfortunately, at the same time the professional is celebrating the new funding and strengthened professional-family relations, a tension is beginning, that in many cases, eventually undermines the positive partnership. This arises from expectations on the part of the professional that may prove overly ambitious and unrealistic. Being accustomed to organizations with well-developed procedures that enable ready response to state contracts, the state-level professional expects the same of the fledgling family organization.

Almost inevitably there are delays, misunderstandings, and lack of fulfillment of specific contract requirements because of a mismatch between the family organization's skills and previous experience and the level of organizational/bureaucratic sophistication that a state contract assumes. Thus, a relationship that begins with the best of intentions on both sides can quickly sour, at times leading to major conflict that is ultimately destructive to a family organization's success in working on behalf of children and their families.

Let us step back and look at the organizational structures that a new family organization or any organization needs to put into place to be successful.

PREPARING FOR LEADERSHIP

The first crucial step is to help ensure strong leadership in a new family organization. My experience is that most new family leaders have little experience leading organizations. This can be a point of collaboration, where the professional working with the organization can help support the leader's development as part of the contractual arrangement.

There are many sources of leadership and organizational development training to help bolster the new executive director's skills to handle her expanded responsibilities. State and federal agencies can further assist family leaders' growth through activities such as creating and nourishing a peer group of new family leaders across states (or other leaders of advocacy and support organizations within a state) for networking and support; encouraging mentor relationships that match new leaders with seasoned leaders who have "been through it all"; and providing resources for site visits so new executive directors can spend a few days at a more established family support organization.

The key ingredients are professionals who are willing to step up to the plate with some investment dollars, and new executive directors who are open to getting this kind of training. These elements are absolutely critical if the organization is to succeed. Neglecting to help prepare the family organization's leader for the challenges is likely to lead to those unequal expectations between family leader and professional leader that cause great harm.

PARENTS AS LEADERS: A MATTER OF BALANCE

The successful parent leaders I have met have a number of skills that serve them well. They have a clear sense of their organization's mission coupled with the ability to articulate it.

This clarity of purpose, along with a passion for the work, is a strength that is perhaps unique to leaders (and some members) of citizen advocacy organizations. Effective parent leaders also possess good people skills and have what appears to be a natural understanding of community organizing that has helped them mobilize families to action on behalf of individual children, to change policies that affect large numbers of children, and even, in some cases, to achieve appropriations from state legislatures.

These skills are most common among the first generation of family organization leaders, whose energy and commitment to the cause, often coupled with righteous anger, initially brings people together. Very often, as the person who created the organization moves on, the successors reflect the kind of leadership needed to stabilize funding and seek new resources. The work seems a bit less personal than is the case with the first-generation leader, and though this means the passion that later leaders possess may not be at the same level, the ability to look beyond one's own situation can be key to long-term effectiveness.

In order to be respected by those outside their organization, family leaders must learn to keep the business side of the work on the table and not personalize it (Heifetz and Linsky, 2002). This is a tall order, as it is generally through years of experience trying to obtain needed services for their own children that family members evolve into leaders of family organizations. And certainly, when it comes to our own children, everything is personal. One step away from our own children are children with a similar disability, which is also very personal. Family organizations often seem to be driven by the motto, "What the system has done to your child could easily be done to my child." Very personal.

It is often said that our greatest strength is also our greatest weakness. We see this dynamic at work when a family leader, rather than view a problem as a matter to resolve through reasoned analysis and a plan of action, takes issues too personally and begins finger-pointing and blaming. At the same time, many well-intentioned professionals have so overdone their efforts to help family organizations that parent leaders no longer value them as vital partners, instead thinking, "If it weren't for so-and-so, we'd be much better off." Neither reputation is necessarily deserved. And either inflating or underestimating the role of professionals can lead to misunderstanding and conflict.

The ability to avoid the personal realm and maintain objectivity can be one of the greatest strengths a family leader can bring to the job. In my experience it is usually those "second-generation" leaders who are able to bring this quality to the organization, largely because they are driven less by passion than the founders usually are. Some family organizations have managed to ensure an objective leader by turning to a more business-oriented individual who may not even be a family member. However, this creates its own problems, when the leader of the family group does not share the sense of having "been there" with the parents who comprise the membership. In the end, a balance between passion and objectivity is generally most desirable. With some training and support, family members who become leaders can reach that middle ground.

Creating a Strong Board

Putting together a dynamic board of directors is important to ensuring the long-term success of a family organization. With regards to building a board, the most common mistake

I have seen is requiring that the board be 100 percent family members. Clearly, a majority of board members need to be family members to guarantee that the organization stays true to its founding mission. However, unless family members can be found with careers in law, accounting, education, and business; management jobs in human service and advocacy organizations; and political clout, it is vital to round out the board with members from a variety of strategic professions.

Decisions can be made more effectively if you can see all the variables that come into play, a kind of "view from the balcony" (Heifetz and Linsky, 2002) with regard to the choices that need to be made in the organization. Family members are often so involved in the day-to-day work of helping individual families that they are working and living in what is described by Heifetz and Linsky as being down on the "dance floor." Their ability to see the big picture is very limited from that vantage point. Board members who work outside this arena, yet have an interest in the organization's mission, can bring that valuable "balcony" view to the table.

A dynamic and diverse board is important for other reasons. Young organizations must ensure that they have supporters who can raise money or have such community-wide influence that having that individual on the board enhances the credibility of the organization. Also, the board can be charged with developing a strategic plan that moves the new family organization to seek funding commensurate with the organizational mission that will help support and strengthen it, both in the short term and over the long haul. This is vital to long-term sustainability for any nonprofit organization.

A Family Organization
that "Gets It"

Happily, in spite of the difficulties inherent in starting a new family support organization, there are examples of successful implementation. One is the Family Advocacy and Support Association (FASA) of Washington DC, a community-based family organization that began without any substantial outside resources and has relied on hard work and camaraderie. FASA began as a support group and over time has developed enough to have a paid executive director and an effectively working board. Several unique features of FASA bear mention. First, its service area is only the District of Columbia and is thus confined to a much smaller geographic area than statewide organizations. Members live quite near one another, and many are friends outside of the organization as well. FASA members come from the community they serve and are culturally and ethnically representative of that community, which is a real strength.

For a number of years FASA resisted affiliation with any national organization, fearing this would take away the sense of independence that members valued. FASA finally decided to join the Federation of Families for Children's Mental Health, yet it has managed to maintain its identity as a family organization that is truly community-based.

FASA has cycled in and out of the federal government's Family Network and Support Grant Program. At times, it has had the $60,000-a-year grant, and at other times, it has not won the grant competition and had to make do without that substantial financial support. However, FASA wisely avoided putting all of its eggs in the "federal grant basket." The organization has thus remained viable even when federal funding was not available. Several factors are involved.

First, FASA stayed lean throughout its early years, relying primarily on volunteers working from home, rather than using grant funds to rent and furnish office space that the organization might not later be able to afford. The Family Network grants have been primarily used for specific initiatives and trainings that require one-time costs yet provide long-term benefits. Further, FASA has built up the goodwill and trust of both government funders and others with the means to contribute. When money is needed for a special project or conference, the organization is able to find the support it needs without moving from its family-focused mission.

Through staying true to its grass-roots beginnings and building a strong and close-knit network of members committed to working on behalf of families, FASA has managed to flourish, both during times when federal funding was a large part of the budget, and when it had to manage without a network grant. Recently, FASA's strong mission and connectedness with the community, coupled with the organization's conscious focus on sustainability and gradual expansion, have garnered a substantial infusion of federal funds, enabling manageable growth of the organization and its system-of-care activities.

FAMILY ORGANIZATIONS IN COMMUNITY-BASED SYSTEMS OF CARE

In 1992, the new federal initiative to provide significant funding to communities ready to create comprehensive systems of care for children with serious emotional disturbance and their families got under way. That first year, four communities received multimillion dollar grants through the Comprehensive Community Mental Health Services for Children and Their Families Program. Seven more were added in fiscal year 1993 and another ten soon after. By 2004, more than eighty communities had been funded all across America. A major requirement was that the funded projects include families in meaningful ways at all levels of system-of-care development.

Those supervising the newly funded projects were in most cases eager to contract with a community-based family organization, to make good on their promises of family involvement. While several communities that received system-of-care grants already had active local family organizations with considerable experience, this was definitely the exception. Most funded communities had, at best, loosely organized support groups.

The new system-of-care communities generally provided family groups with large contracts—from $100,000 to $500,000. Even at the lower end, this is typically more than the entire budget of community organizations just starting out. In many cases, the contract from the recently awarded system-of-care grant was the first real money a family organization had ever received.

Far from enabling an organic, gradual development, which was the path successfully taken by community-based organizations such as FASA in Washington DC, parents were faced with the daunting task of pulling together a formal local family organization capable of carrying out multiple tasks amid a sharp increase in activity around building a community-based system of care. The expectations on the part of the system-of-care project leaders were commensurate with the amount of money provided. The contracts nearly always required the local family organization to plan and implement a range of complex tasks, including care coordination, individual advocacy for children and families, and data collection and evaluation. As many of these organizations were just opening their doors, they were expected to hire and train staff to handle the multiple responsibilities and begin delivering services often before they even had time to put an infrastructure into place.

This lack of readiness meant that the excitement and high hopes for effective professional-family collaboration that accompanied the awarding of the multimillion dollar system-of-care grants often gave way to difficulties, some with disastrous consequences, once the work began.

Caution: Money Plus Inexperience Can Be a Harmful Mix

It is critical for new family organizations to take on only as much as they can handle. The promise of new money is very appealing to any small agency, but the potential for failure is high if an organization accepts significant funds without the capacity to competently deliver the required services or account for the funds. This caution applies equally to those holding the purse strings. Communities receiving large system-of-care grants are often times eager to show their willingness to work with families as full partners. Many make the mistake of offering start-up family organizations enormous sums at the get-go that the organizations are unprepared to use wisely, given their lack of administrative structures and management experience.

Remember the "expectations" rule, which will quickly come into play once a contract is signed and funding is authorized. I have seen numerous family organizations and the professional leadership of the new community-based systems of care battle one another over accusations of poor performance, lack of accountability, unacceptable accounting practices, and other sub-performance allegations. I have seen family leaders fired for alleged mismanagement of funds and contracts ended prematurely or substantially reduced by the state funding agency because of allegations that contract funds were inadequately managed.

What follows is loss of trust between the two entities, reduced contract amounts, firing of family executive directors, removal of board chairs of family organizations, and a general disintegration of the relationship between professional and family leaders. Lasting harm is done to the entire system-of-care development process. In the end, no one is quite sure why things went so far wrong. Yet, if one steps back, it is clear that too much responsibility was thrust upon the family organization too quickly. There was inadequate time to build an organization before launching into service provision for the new system of care.

I am hard pressed to think of many successes when a newly formed family organization engages with a richly funded yet new community-based system of care, unless the money and tasks of the contract match the developmental level of the family organization. One approach that has worked is providing a modest contract to the family organization early on, with clear achievable tasks, and future funding dependent on successful completion of these tasks. Another effective strategy that several grant communities have used is to initially give money to family organizations aimed solely at helping them build the organization, with no service component attached. Funding for services is provided once the organization has gone through a developmental process, such as executive director training, building a working board, and establishing accounting systems, thus demonstrating readiness to play an active role in system-of-care activities. In my experience, this gradual approach has paid off in terms of a family organization that gains the trust and respect of other project partners, and eventually has had significant impact on the system of care and the families served.

Strengths Unique to Local Family Organizations

Perhaps what most separates many local family organizations from their statewide counterparts is cultural diversity. The statewide family organizations are nearly all overwhelmingly white and middle class in membership, while local, community-based parent organizations are much more likely to reflect the racial, cultural, language, and socioeconomic characteristics of the communities where they are based. This is a most valuable feature, enabling local organizations to reach out and connect with their communities' children with serious emotional disturbance and their families in ways less diverse organizations cannot. Their cultural competence is probably one of the local family organizations' most appealing aspects of new systems of care. This also speaks to the importance of cultural competence training for state organizations and the need to look at how much effort is put into ensuring that the state family organization is sufficiently diverse.

Community-based family organizations are generally better suited than state family organizations to supervise family staff contracted to do work in local systems of care. I recall one state where the local system of care contracted with the state family organization to provide care coordinators. It soon became clear that the state organization was not properly supervising staff from its offices many miles from the local system of care. Issues of staff meeting attendance, providing regular staff support, and making sure the contractor was getting what was needed and agreed to became logistical problems for the supervising organization. In another state where the state organization was contracted to do work for a local system of care, the state organization consistently hired staff with little sensitivity to the cultural dynamics of the community. After three attempts to hire a local leader from the state capital, the local system of care finally contracted directly with the now more seasoned local family organization. A family leader from the community was hired and the leadership problem was resolved.

Finally, who can better understand local issues than the people who work, play, and live in the community? Long-time residents are naturally most familiar with the cultural, social, political, religious, and community issues that drive decisions on behalf of their children, as well as for the larger group of families with children who have mental health needs.

THE VALUE ADDED FROM STATEWIDE ORGANIZATIONS

Statewide family organizations can be very useful to local efforts by bringing a new or broader perspective to an issue, whereas local folks may get "stuck" because of their closeness to the community. It's that "balcony" perspective mentioned earlier (Heifetz and Linsky, 2002). Also, the political connections of the state organization can be very helpful in supporting the work of community groups. The relationship between the two organizations can be complementary, supporting families at a personal level and affecting policies, programs, and funding as well, through the political clout a strong statewide body can wield.

Leaders should focus on developing the relationship between community and state organizations when times are good. Attention too often first turns to the relationships between state and local family organizations only when tension arises. We need more preventive work on building positive ties between them prior to a potential crisis. This will provide a cushion of mutual trust and goodwill to see them through times that test their mutual support.

Supervising Staff
Working in Systems of Care

More and more, staffs of local family organizations are being hired to play significant roles within community-based systems of care. The question of who supervises their work has become an issue of concern and debate across the country. Early on, a number of parents hired by family organizations went to work within systems of care with supervision provided by the local government agencies leading the projects. This did not often work out well, as family members felt torn between the two organizations and pulled between sometimes conflicting rules and procedures. In most cases, after some difficult negotiating, the supervision was moved to the family organization, resolving the problem. Now most family organizations have learned that it is important to maintain supervisory control over their staff, even as they work in close partnership with the agencies leading the system-of-care activities.

Another supervisory strategy has been to hire a family

member to join the government team overseeing local system-of-care development. Where this has occurred, the new family voice has been crucial in shifting agency thinking about families in a positive way.

This approach has been very effective at the federal level as well. The Child, Adolescent and Family Branch at the Center for Mental Health Services has had the wonderful benefit of consistently having at least one parent activist as a member since 1993. The parent's role is to represent the family point of view in discussions, ensure strong family representation at all federally sponsored meetings and change how organizations talk to and about parents.

This is an important position, but also one that can be very difficult to perform year in and year out. In organizations that are not sensitive to family issues, the designated family member ends up having to confront many issues that are being knowingly or unknowingly framed to diminish the family voice. The position within a bureaucracy can be isolating for a parent, and the constant confrontation that goes along with the position can take its toll. My sense is that parents taking on such a role should expect that three to five years is a reasonable tenure, given the constant pressures they face.

RIGHTING WRONGS TAKES WORK

We have talked about misaligned expectations between the funding source and family organization, the tendency to over-personalize the work, and reliance on only one funding source for the survival of the organization as potential sources of conflict. If these issues are not dealt with productively, they can have disastrous consequences for the long-term relationship between family organizations and those funding them. As mentioned earlier, I have seen this lead to disruption of the organization's activities, dismissal of the director and staff, the end of contracts that have sustained an organization, and, finally, a sense of bewilderment and dismay at how this sad state of affairs came to be.

No matter how difficult things become, if the family organization and the funding agency are willing to try to work it out, I believe that problems can be resolved. There are several essential steps. First, both parties need people who are "on the balcony," who are not involved in the conflict, and thus can look at the big picture with some objectivity and provide a balanced understanding of factors involved. These may be board members, an organizational development consultant, a trusted supervisor, or a confidant who will "tell it like it is" (Heifetz and Linsky, 2002). It is important to resist turning only to people who will confirm one's notions about the situation, even though that would feel affirming and comfortable. In the end, this is no time for passion and blame; reasoned thinking is what's needed.

All parties need to commit to the process of thinking through the situation, seeking objective viewpoints and analyzing what can be done to improve matters. Even with the best of efforts on these fronts, it may not be possible to overcome the pain that comes from failing to forge and maintain a good relationship with agency leadership. Again, it is best to not personalize the situation. And second, we must do all we can do before totally retreating from a working relationship.

Mediation as a Promising Strategy

A key piece missing in many communities is people trained to mediate problems that may arise between parent organizations and the professional organizations that fund them. Given that these professional/family problems are playing out around the country, with clashes becoming almost commonplace, we must deal with these situations in a thoughtful and methodical way.

Beyond those people who can help us see a situation from the "balcony" perspective, I propose that we train pairs of parents and professionals to serve as official mediators to defuse crisis situations. These pairs would be highly skilled in conflict resolution and knowledgeable about intraorganizational problems. Formal mediation training should be provided by a neutral outside organization. I have stressed the importance of keeping the work on the table and not personalizing it. These pairs need to be very sophisticated to make sure this happens in their work with communities. Providing this kind of objective eye aimed at constructive solutions could make a real difference in bringing organizations back to a commitment to work together.

Concluding Thoughts

I hope that I have helped clarify the complexities of the relationship between family organizations and the professionals with whom they contract to work. There are no clear "good and bad guys" here. Almost all are well-meaning people who get caught in change dynamics that can make life complicated. Inherent in the difficulties that arise are differing assumptions, power relationships, skills, and priorities regarding the work at hand. Each of these issues can either bind the work of both groups closer or pull them apart. Sadly, the latter has been all too common as I have watched the system of care and parent involvement efforts move forward.

It is clearly a defining time for creating community-based systems of care. As scores of communities have joined in this effort, I sometimes fear that we have not grown along with the tremendous expansion of system-of-care activity and funding. If we choose to work as we did when there was little money to build family organizations and organized systems of care, we will ultimately fail. Being a Vermont resident, I like to use the example of Ben & Jerry's Ice Cream. Had young Ben Cohen and Jerry Greenfield not taken the steps, including some risky ones, to turn their popular scoop shop in an abandoned gas station into a sophisticated manufacturing business, it would have languished and eventually perished.

Growing pains are a difficult yet inevitable part of success. If a new approach shows promise, people get excited about it. More resources are invested and more folks climb on board. The process becomes more complex and risks losing the passion and creativity that drove the original idea. Solutions lie in the kinds of questions we can generate that get us to open up and explore options for new directions. I trust that we will make the necessary changes to enable systems of care that are truly responsive to and representative of families. My hope is that we can maximize the benefits to children with serious emotional disturbance, and their families and communities, and minimize the conflict and pain that accompany all significant change efforts.

REFERENCE

Heifetz, R.A. & M. Linsky (2002).
Leadership on the Line. Cambridge, MA: Harvard University Press.

Chapter Five:

Leadership in Systems of Care—

The Heifetz and Linsky Model in Action

*There are risks and costs
to a program of action. But they are
far less than the long-range risks
and costs of comfortable inaction.*

—John F. Kennedy

The role of leaders in new systems of care is to manage and steer communities through what is often a rocky and stressful change process. I came to understand the crucial nature of leadership in systems of care through visiting many of the communities receiving federal grants to develop local systems.

At the same time, I became immersed in the work of Dr. Ronald Heifetz and Marty Linsky through participating in their weeklong leadership training seminar at Harvard and follow-up reading on their illuminating theory of leadership. This chapter is an attempt to fuse the leadership theory put forth by Heifetz and Linsky with the leadership work being done across the country in the process of building and maintaining systems of care for children who need multiple services and supports.

We all know that the system reform necessary to build and sustain a system of care is tremendous. I have always said that it is the hardest work you will come to love. Any one of the system-of-care principles can take a lifetime to implement. Think about it: cultural competence, parent and family involvement, home- and community-based services for all children with a mental health disorder, individualized care, interagency collaboration, strength-based assessments. Is there a simple one among the group?

LEADERSHIP AS AN INVESTMENT

Given the tremendous challenge of system change, how much time and effort have we devoted to ensuring that those who take on the mantle of leadership are prepared for what their efforts in a change process will bring? Juxtapose the public investment in leadership to what occurs in the private sector. The business community spends millions of dollars on the next generation of leaders. When an individual rises to the top of a private sector organization, he or she is a known quantity in whom the company has invested substantially to assure success. Newly appointed leaders have been groomed to understand quite clearly what it takes to move an organization forward, to inspire the organization to help all employees achieve great performance in their jobs (Belasco and Stayer, 1993).

Compare this with the public sector, where the investment in leadership is minimal, with the result that many of our public sector leaders are hurt by the change process and do not understand why they are not effective. Some of them experience debilitating isolation and character assassinations. Too many leave their positions under pressure or just throw in the towel and depart with a terrible sense of failure.

Few public sector leaders succeed in helping their communities move through the change process without great personal and professional pain. Many wonder how and why they have moved from a time of community success and harmony, often being greatly appreciated for their previous work, to a point where it seems that everyone would be happy if they left—tomorrow. The risks associated with change can paralyze even the most open-minded change-oriented communities and spell trouble for those leading the community effort.

The following tale, which underscores the difficulty of leading change efforts, prompted me to do something about preparing leaders for the challenges they face. I was visiting a system-of-care community where the state director of children's mental health was designing a dynamic managed-care system that entailed major fiscal and programmatic changes. The new system would provide a range of innovative service and infrastructure improvements, but required providers to move from a paper accounting system to a computer-based system for tracking services and dollars spent on children. It was a huge step forward for the entire system.

Change will bring resistance no matter how beneficial the idea is for the community. Fearful of how the restructuring might upset the current system (which though inefficient and ineffective was known and comfortable) some community leaders began rumors aimed at hurting the children's mental health director. A scrap of information was turned into a damning story with little factual basis but potent in its power to undercut the leader's legitimacy. When sectors of a community are committed to "avoiding the work," any strategy to keep the status quo will be used (Heifetz and Linsky, 2002). Watching this process in action made it clear to me that something had to be done to help our leaders and communities if systems of care were to succeed.

For a moment let's go back to the basics of what it takes to be an effective leader. Though it may seem so, leaders are not born. They achieve mastery of many skills by learning from experiences, practicing, and trying again and again. We too often tend to compare ourselves to renowned world leaders and find ourselves lacking. We forget that individuals like Martin Luther King Jr., Mahatma Gandhi, and Margaret Mead spent many years honing their leadership skills in less public ways until they began to have an impact on the larger community, and eventually the world.

We all need to ask ourselves, "Who am I? What values do I hold most dear? What makes me feel that life is worth living and that it's great to be alive? Whom do I most respect? What values do they hold? What is my purpose in life?" There are many ways to move into this part of ourselves, from guided imagery to values clarification exercises. Regardless of the process you use, it is important to do that internal work. Your vision will come from understanding your values and passions in life. There is no shortcut to this part of the work.

"OUT OF TRIBE" EXPERIENCES

In a fascinating analysis of one hundred social change leaders, *Common Fire* (Daloz, Keen, Keen & Parks,1996), the authors found that the leaders all described ". . . some event or experience of 'otherness' that jolted their idea of who they were and where they stood in the world, challenging their previously held assumptions about who was 'one of us' and who was not." In some cases, this meant spending time in a new environment, where they came into contact with unfamiliar places, people, and customs. These leaders had visited another country as children or teenagers, or attended summer camp with children of a different social class, culture, or race, or spent time in another part of the country where they felt quite different from those around them. The rest of the leaders learned about otherness through becoming close with a classmate from a different social class, cultural, or ethnic group and getting to know his or her family and neighborhood, or volunteering to work with children with disabilities and thus learning to overcome their fear of differences.

These "out of tribe" experiences broadened these future leaders' views of the world. They realized that there is more than one "right" way to live, and they became open to valuing the diversity of our world. I suspect that if we all had that kind of experience the issues of cultural competence would be much easier to address.

Recently, a colleague invited me to attend the closing ceremony for a group of sixty youths who had been together for three weeks. The participants were intentionally selected so that twenty were Jewish, twenty were Catholic, and twenty were Protestant. They spent this time together to learn more about their own faiths and at the same time learn more about the faiths of the other two groups. As I was sitting through a wonderful variety show that they had put together as their closing statement to themselves, the faculty, and their families, I couldn't help but recall the description of experiencing otherness that I'd read about.

Late that evening, as I was talking to a rabbi who was involved with the youths, I mentioned the book *Common Fire* and the notion of "out of tribe" experiences. He immediately responded, "Would you like to meet one of the authors?" "Absolutely," I replied, "but how could you make that happen?" The rabbi said, "He's right over there," and pointed across the room. And there indeed was one of the four authors! He was at this event to evaluate the young participants' experience for the same reason I was thinking about it. He was assessing to what extent the coming together of these youths from different backgrounds opened them up to a new world view. I was stunned at the synchronicity of the experience and excited to be able to tell the author that I use his book over and over. I asked, "How many copies of this wonderful book have you sold?" I assumed it would be a big hit. He quietly said, "thirteen thousand." I left thinking with regret about this gem of a book that so few have had the pleasure of reading.

Although the leaders in *Common Fire* learned to value differentness early in life, I am convinced that it is never too late to gain from the process of spending time out of our comfort zones. I think it is important to stretch yourself no matter what your age. Get out and live a full life! You will be a better leader for it.

FINDING SHELTER IN OUR SANCTUARIES

The word "sanctuary" conjures a place, but in Heifetz's (1994) view, sanctuaries are those activities that we do just for ourselves. Sanctuaries are critical to restoring our energy and nurturing our passions in life. There are no expectations for your sanctuary other than that it is something you enjoy and have readily available. The list of sanctuaries is infinite: some of those commonly mentioned are painting, cooking, gardening, lunch with friends, or a walk in the country.

Unfortunately, our sanctuaries are too often sacrificed for another meeting or activity related to our work. We do this at our peril, as illustrated by the next story, a common one among our system-of-care leadership. This example demonstrates the dedication and drive that leaders need to build successful systems of care, while underscoring the fact that if we try too hard or work too long without rejuvenating ourselves we can actually become an impediment to the change process.

A particular community leader had been trying hard to bring all the stakeholders together to blend funds, create collaborative services, and begin including families as partners in the work of building the community's system of care. He found great resistance in every step forward by the very people who had said for years that the children's mental health system needed major improvements. He met with agency heads individually, added financial incentives to move them past their turf issues, and tried a variety of other strategies to encourage them to collaborate. However, despite all of his best efforts, those in charge still resisted system change.

After a few years of this frustrating work, the leader was exhausted. He had nothing left in his tank. Guess what? Community stakeholders were finally ready to make great strides forward in all of the areas that he had initially wanted them to embrace. Incredibly, it was now the leader who did not want them to change, for fear that any change would bring him more work. His was a classic case of "burnout." This individual actually went out of his way to try to stop others from moving forward because he feared he could not do the work to support the change that they finally were committed to make happen! What is wrong with this picture?

In his passion for the work, the leader lost himself in the process. He abandoned his sanctuaries, sacrificing his vital time for renewal in favor of that one extra meeting, that one more unreasonable deadline that he *had* to meet. If we neglect our sanctuaries, we risk becoming like this leader: an impediment to making change happen.

Another story I tell is of the person who declared at a leadership training that his sanctuary was his work. He enthusiastically exclaimed, "I'm a 24/7 work person and I live for work!" He loved every minute of it, he declared. In spite of our coaching him to try to identify a sanctuary outside of work, it was no use. The sad part of the story is that funding for his program had ended and the center where he worked would most likely close, leaving him without the job he so adored. This dramatic change for someone who has put all of their eggs in that work basket can be devastating.

The Person Versus the Position— Watch Out for the Merge

Rarely do people see us for who we are when we are in our various leadership roles. People are taken by the power and image of that role. Do not confuse how people act with you when you are in your leadership role with what they think of you as an ordinary person after you leave the role at work. If you are starting to think that how people act with you in your leadership role is how they see you as a person, beware. This is usually a sign that you are overextended in your work life and are beginning to merge who you are with what you do at work. If you are having trouble with this concept try the following.

At a large meeting where you are known as a leader, take note of how people treat you: what they tell you, how they address you, how they look at you, etc. If this meeting is in a hotel or conference center where another conference where you are unknown is in progress, drop in on that meeting. Introduce yourself to several participants. Observe how people respond to you, watch their body language, see who introduces themselves to you. It shouldn't take long to get a sense of the difference. You haven't changed at all, but the status you hold with one group of people by virtue of your position is entirely missing with the second group. Those in the first group view you within the context of your position, while the new people simply see you as a person they do not know, judging you solely by what you look like, say, and do upon first meeting them.

People see the position more than they see the person, and will treat you accordingly. If you are mistakenly viewing yourself only by how people respond to you in your formal position, it may be time for a vacation, time to rekindle your sanctuaries and live your life beyond work.

Shared Vision

Let's assume that you have a good sense of who you are and what you value and have found the kind of work that reflects those things about yourself. The next key piece of the leader's work is to develop a shared vision. As with most goals, this is easier said than done. Probably the most important skill needed to achieve a shared vision is *listening*. Seek out both those who are doing the work and those potentially benefiting from the work of building a system of care, and then listen. Ask questions like, "What are your goals for children who have a mental health disorder and their families? What works in the current system? What is not working? What would you do differently if you could wave a magic wand and make it happen?"

Listening to the hopes and dreams of various stakeholders and packaging their thoughts into a vision that can be understood and embraced by all concerned with systems of care is the work of the leader. Think of the vision put forth by Martin Luther King Jr. back in 1963 in his "I Have a Dream" speech. King was so powerful because he spoke to what we all want for our children, our communities, and our nation. Shared visions are hard to kill, as the whole community is invested in turning them into reality. Visions that come down from the top are rarely successful in motivating a community to action. In fact, top-down visions that do not respect or reflect the views of the people for whom the vision is designed make people feel put upon and less engaged.

HOLDING ENVIRONMENT: CREATING A SAFE PLACE

Another piece of the work of the leader is to create a "holding environment" (Heifetz, 1994). A holding environment is just that, an environment, rather than an actual location. This is the term Heifetz coined for a place where all the stakeholders can gather and feel safe enough to talk about their value conflicts and their disagreements with how things are going. Individuals can openly share ideas for new ways of doing things, along with questions and concerns.

It is the leader's job to create a climate of safe dialogue and discourse, and to manage the holding environment. If things are too placid the leader may need to infuse some new ways of thinking to shake things up a bit. New information can do this. Conversely, the leader may need to cool down the atmosphere if the change is taking place so quickly that those who are part of the system become overanxious. Too much change and the community will not be able to handle it; there will be pressure to go back to the way things were. Too little change and the community becomes stale and nothing moves forward, even when it is apparent that current strategies are not working well for children and their families or for the community at large.

As we began our system-of-care strategic planning in Vermont, we put together an advisory board of key stakeholders across the state. We invited advocates, legislators, parents, service providers, state child-serving agencies, and academics. Although I didn't yet know this term, this was a holding environment where these disparate parties could come together and safely debate and discuss controversial issues.

One of the group's first goals was to tackle the many definitions of "serious emotional disturbance." At that time, a child could be served in one system, only to be denied services in another system because of different criteria. This was a tremendous obstacle to cross-agency collaboration on behalf of children and families.

You can well imagine how this played out in the group. Some members of the advisory committee, mostly advocates and parents, wanted the broadest definition possible. Meanwhile, the state agency representatives worried that the broader the definition, the more financial and legal responsibility they would hold.

My role, as the designated leader, was to manage the debate engendered by these different views within the holding environment, with the goal of coming to a resolution that would result in more interagency collaboration. After a full board discussion that brought out many of the issues, a subcommittee was formed to work on a definition and report back to the full board at various decision-making points. The subcommittee first gathered all applicable state and federal definitions of serious emotional disturbance, then examined the similarities and the differences. The discussion continued for eighteen months in a back-and-forth process between the subcommittee and the board, with input from various state agencies. The key to effectiveness was that at no time did anyone condemn or personalize a particular stand. All involved came to understand that there was really no right or wrong, but rather differing viewpoints on the matter. After setting up the framework for doing the work, my primary job was to just keep a watchful eye over the process.

Eventually the subcommittee proposed a definition of serious emotional disturbance that was broader than the federal Department of Education's. Any child meeting the state definition would receive services regardless of whether they were eligible for special education under federal guidelines. Agreement was unanimous, and within the year that definition was passed into Vermont state law as Act 264. It still exists today, some seventeen years later, as a landmark piece of state legislation.

A lasting byproduct of this work was a tremendous amount of goodwill and ownership of the eventual success by everyone involved. The advisory board became so invested in systems of care that its collective power helped forge groundbreaking interagency partnerships, grant opportunities, blended funding efforts, and parent involvement opportunities. If a leader can create and support the holding environment, change can happen in a deep, meaningful way with few participants feeling they lost and nearly all feeling they have gained something of value.

Controlling the "Temperature" of the Holding Environment

The role of leadership in times of change is to modulate the "temperature" of the environment to respond to the situation. Too cool and nothing changes, too hot and it causes anxiety among the players and destabilizes the work environment. In the following case I consciously set out to heat things up to open a group to new ways of thinking so they could keep current with changes in the field and actively model system-of-care values in their work with communities.

When I went to Washington DC as head of the Child, Adolescent and Family Branch of the Center for Mental Health Services, I found homeostasis among the national leaders who had been working together for some years. Glaring omissions in cultural competence and family involvement from my outsider's perspective were not at all evident to this group of long-time colleagues. It was my job to poke and pry. Each of my incursions into what was missing was met with much dissatisfaction among the group. Yet I knew if we were going to grow and change, someone needed to start pointing out the short-comings, question the status quo, and push the group members to realize they were missing important pieces of the puzzle in their work with communities.

The confrontations were difficult: some staffers left, others complied with my efforts to strengthen the areas that needed improvement, and several people even jumped into the work with a renewed spirit. Most of what I suggested was initially met with resistance, but the staff members who stayed eventually recognized the need to change. In the end, I know that the product they delivered was much closer to what the communities they served wanted and needed. This was a case that called for heating up the temperature, which creates discomfort, but can lead to much better outcomes than "going along to get along."

TECHNICAL AND ADAPTIVE CHALLENGES

Much of what you go through in building a system of care is what Heifetz and Linsky refer to as an "adaptive challenge" (Heifetz and Linsky, 2002). Adaptive challenges are changes that require a shift in values. For example, if you were taught that parents are the primary cause for their child's mental health disorder and thus are the problem, it will require a value shift to have you embrace parents as partners and part of the solution. If you sincerely believe that the best place to deliver clinical services is within the confines of your office, then no course or information is going to help you decide that practicing in schools and children's homes is the best way to go. These situations each present an adaptive challenge.

Heifetz and Linsky make a clear distinction between adaptive and what they term "technical challenges." If the change required is of a technical nature, then a solid training curriculum can address the skill gap. Technical challenges are generally much easier to resolve than are adaptive challenges as they simply require making available the information that an individual, agency, or system may need to do the job well.

It is important that leaders learn to identify whether challenges they face are of an adaptive or technical nature. If, for example, you face the adaptive challenge of resolving the fact that your clinicians would rather do their clinical work in their offices than in homes and schools, and you respond by having them take a course in systems of care, you have missed the point about their resistance to working differently. You will have as little success persuading them to change their approach after the course as you had before it, since the issue is one of a value the clinicians hold versus providing them with needed information.

This is where the holding environment comes to bear. A more effective strategy than providing technical help through training would be to provide a place where the therapists can vent their frustration at having to do things differently. Information can be a part of the approach, but first we need to help people become open to even listening to the new information being put forth.

The reverse is also true. We might assume that since few parents of children with a disability have a PhD in Experimental Psychology, they therefore have no interest in research. We then incorrectly decide that we are facing an adaptive challenge. In fact, many parents may want to learn about relevant research. What they need is help of a technical nature—a basic understanding of evaluation and research tools in user-friendly terms so they can use the information wisely for their children and for other system change efforts. By missing the kind of challenge facing us we can spend countless hours and a lot of money looking at the wrong solution.

There are issues that present both technical and adaptive challenges. I think of cultural competence as a prime example. Some leaders find it most comfortable to stay within their own cultural group and will end up hiring staff that reflect their own background, excluding those of different ethnic or cultural heritage. What starts out as providing a sense of safety and security to the leader may quickly end up as culturally incompetent work when that staff now must interact with a community that may be from a totally different cultural background. We can quite readily teach leaders such techniques as marketing to attract applicants of diverse backgrounds, offering cultural competency training to current staff, and including people of different ethnic and cultural groups on the board. The adaptive challenge is somehow getting these same leaders to actually embrace the principles of cultural competence and be open to having a culturally diverse staff, to understand why it's important in their work rather than just understand the technical steps involved. Once someone is open to the value of cultural competence, it becomes a matter of giving them all the tools necessary to do the work in an excellent manner.

CULTURAL DIFFERENCES IN LEADERSHIP

It is important to also think of leadership in the context of culture. As ethnic and cultural factors play a role in all aspects of systems of care, they are naturally present in leadership styles as well. I will never forget the conversation I had with a well-known and respected Native American leader who told me that leaders in his community would be less respected if they showed emotion. Given my Italian-American heritage, only two generations removed from Italy, I might approach the leadership role a bit differently! That is what makes America beautiful, while also making it so important that we become sensitive to the unique factors that come into play when we are working with culturally diverse groups. This doesn't mean that you give up who you are in relating to others as a leader. It does require that you become aware of and respect the cultural and ethnic qualities of the groups you are working with.

My hope is to have leadership embrace the wonderful diversity of the world we live in. Use this critical piece of our work to break through fear, be courageous, and take risks. Within this one aspect of systems of care, you have the opportunity to be the best leader you can be.

COURAGE AND RISK-TAKING

Two other key aspects of leadership are risk-taking and courage. Courage has everything to do with knowing your purpose in life, understanding your passions, and being willing to follow your heart to do what is right for you and your community. Many times the courageous leader says and does the things that others are feeling but are afraid to act upon. They are the ones willing to "step into the void" (Heifetz, 1994). They cannot predict what will happen, but they know it is the right thing to do.

A brave parent ventures a statement at a policy meeting with agency heads that will eventually result in improved policies for children with special needs. A mental health planner insists that parents be included as partners in all aspects of system-of-care development. An agency director advocates for a new emphasis on cultural competence after seeing few people of color involved in supporting children and families in communities that are culturally diverse. The possibilities are endless, but it is clear that in system change, courage is a necessary ingredient if we are going to move our communities forward.

Risk-taking is a learned behavior, closely related to courage. True leaders must be able to accept a certain amount of risk. A highly risk-averse person will do whatever it takes to maintain the status quo, even if that means ignoring new circumstances that require adaptations if the organization is to thrive. These individuals too often hold back their organizations.

On the other hand, there is certainly something to be said for caution on a leader's part. Individuals highly attracted to risk will too often put their agency and its staff in harm's way, based on their "no guts, no glory" approach to every challenge. These leaders tend to create organizations characterized by a high level of anxiety, as they are always taking chances, funding more positions than they have money for while hoping for an infusion of new funds, radically changing everything from year to year in a quest for innovation, and so on.

I advise new leaders to evaluate how comfortable they are taking risks. If you feel that it would benefit your work to increase your ability to take on risk, it is important to push yourself up the ladder of risk-taking behavior, but not so far up that you are unnerved by the thought of the impending risk you will face. As with a ladder, take one step at a time.

If you rate risk-taking behavior from one to ten and decide that you are a "level three" risk-taker, you probably want to take a risk that is a level four or five. Trying to take a risk that is in the level seven area will cause too much anxiety, and you will probably fail, resulting in your being even less of a risk-taker in the future. This applies in reverse for high-level risk-takers. They should step down the ladder gradually. If they drastically reduce their level of risk, they will become so bored with the results that they are likely to resume taking great risks.

Another point about risk-taking is that you do not have to be the only one putting yourself on the line. Others around you might be best suited for a particular risk. The key is to know and understand yourself, stretch yourself, and partner.

TOOL KIT FOR THRIVING IN CHAOS

In this last section let us consider other crucial pieces of the tool kit. We have already talked about the need for sanctuaries.

ALLIES VERSUS CONFIDANTS

Excellent leaders understand the difference between two types of work relationships that Heifetz aptly labels "allies" and "confidants" (Heifetz, 1994). Partners are key to enabling us to move forward in developing a system of care. While effective leaders develop productive working relationships with a number of individuals, it is important to keep in mind that most of these people are allies and not confidants. They are key people in your work life, but their loyalty to you is very much based on the issue of the day. They may be your strongest supporters on a major issue where you both have much at stake. However, beware of expecting them to come through for you when it is not to their benefit. We all serve in the role of allies, aligning with those who have like interests to push forward particular agendas, and then backing off on other issues where our involvement is not likely to help our own agency or career. We are likely to have scores of people we consider allies.

Confidants, on the other hand, are few and far between. We generally have at most a handful of people in our lives who are true confidants. Your chief confidant may be your spouse or partner. Your confidants may work in the same field but live thousands of miles away, or may be close friends not in any way connected to your work.

The main criterion distinguishing confidants is that you can be sure that whatever you tell them remains with them. Additionally, true confidants are loyal whether they agree with you or not. They are also willing and able to give you direct feedback on what they are seeing. Confidants are there for you whenever you need them. You can vent your frustration about a trying individual or situation and know that the information will stay with the confidant and will never come back to haunt you.

A confidant is someone to whom you automatically reach out when you've had a particularly bad day or are faced with a thorny decision. Confidants are also the people with whom you share your triumphs, knowing they are always rooting for you and are thrilled when you succeed. Confidants are special people in our lives. We all need to nurture these valuable relationships that help sustain us through the challenges of leading.

A problem occurs when we confuse the two groups and treat an ally as a confidant, then feel betrayed when he or she turns out not to be the latter. Because your allies are with you only on certain issues and may well be against you on others, they will feel free to use information to hurt you that you have shared based on your assumption that you were dealing with a confidant. We have probably all made this mistake; the consequences are often painful. You quickly begin to see why presidents and other top leaders make sure that close confidants are always at hand.

I have been asked if your supervisor can be your confidant. My usual answer is that this is probably not the safest person to use for this purpose, given the power differential and the fact that they have to oversee and evaluate your work. However, there are exceptions to this rule. Some of us have been fortunate to have had supervisors in our careers who served as valuable mentors and role models and whom we could always trust to act in our best interest.

DISCOVERING YOUR OWN BALCONY

The next tool for effective leadership in systems of care is allowing yourself time to get up on the "balcony" (Heifetz, 1994). Heifetz's notion of a balcony is the process of temporarily removing yourself from the day-to-day operations and taking a broad overview of the landscape that you are dealing with. When we are in the midst of the work it is hard to see all the variables that make up a particular situation. Heifetz likens it to a dance floor, with you being one of the dancers. From this perspective, it is nearly impossible to see all of the different situations that are occurring at a given moment.

Now leave the dance floor and imagine walking up to a balcony overlooking the floor. From here you can see everything: who is dancing, who is standing on the edge of the dance floor, who never gets asked to dance, who may be attempting to cut in on another's partner, and so on. In our work, leaders need to take this vantage point. From the balcony, you may see that you are perhaps missing an important stakeholder, you might notice that a particular individual comes to meetings but is not invested in the work, or an agency is pushing so hard that it is moving the system in ways that are alienating others. It is only on the balcony that you can begin to see these things play out.

One of the easiest times to be on the balcony is when you first enter a new job and are not yet accustomed to "dancing" with your new partners. I can remember first starting my federal position and readily seeing things that did not match with system-of-care principles. For example, in planning for a major conference I noticed that parents were not at the table for crucial decisions, but were being met with separately. Also, I noticed that a proposed advisory group did not represent the cultural diversity that was important to the work we were trying to do with cultural competence in systems of care. It was easy for me to recognize these lapses given my newness to the position. It was far more difficult to get those who had been working together on systems-of-care planning issues for several years to step back onto the balcony and see these as problems that needed addressing.

Another piece of the early balcony work was noticing that there was no mechanism for federal agencies to come together and discuss how they could collaborate across agency lines on behalf of the mental health needs of children and families. Out of that balcony view the Federal/National Partnership for Children's Mental Health was created. Over the years, this group developed numerous interagency agreements and joint grant announcements and won two Vice Presidential Hammer Awards for government innovations and efficiencies.

After you have been in a job for a while, you will not be able to rely on retaining such a clear balcony view, as you are now closely involved in the action on the dance floor. You will need to think of a place or activity that will help you get up on that balcony regularly. Maybe it is a quiet time in your office, on a walk, or even when you are exercising. (You are exercising daily, right?) Whatever it is that takes you to the balcony, it is important to climb those stairs regularly.

If you have been in your position for a year or more, the balcony can help with another dimension of your work. It can be a place to look over the system you have helped create and reflect on how much has been achieved. How few times do we ever stop and see the great work that has been done? When times get tough in systems change work, it is easy to get caught up in the day-to-day frustrations and forget how much you have accomplished over time. In fact, if you do not stop to take a look at what you have been able to do, you will lose that sense of timing and rhythm of when to move forward on initiating the next piece of system change. Step back and celebrate group and individual achievements. Hold ceremonies or use parts of conferences to acknowledge good work and even small successes.

MENTORS

Mentors play an important part in our work life at all ages. When the one hundred leaders of social change analyzed in *Common Fire* were asked, "What key factors came to play an important part in why you chose to devote your life to social change?" one of the common denominators was the role of mentors (Daloz, Keen, Keen & Parks. 1996). Marian Wright Edelman, founder and president of the Children's Defense Fund, has written that her mentors were like lanterns guiding her path through her work and spiritual development (Edelman, 1999). Mentors embody those characteristics that we want for ourselves. In this pioneer work of creating new structures for providing services and supports for children in their home and community, mentors can be significant in helping find solutions to difficult problems.

"TRUSTING YOUR GUT"

As I mentioned earlier, one of the important aspects of leadership is trusting your own decision-making abilities. I usually refer to this as "trusting your gut." Gathering all the information you need to make a thoughtful decision is crucial, seeking counsel is important, and knowing where you and the system stand with regard to being able to manage the current level of change-related stress is also important. Some of the decisions will be hard to make and may in fact trigger much consternation and fallout, including people disliking you. But leaders must make decisions, and I encourage you to trust yourself in this process. It is better to make a decision that you can personally stand by and defend if that time comes, than to make one based on someone else's thoughts that may be harder to support.

FOCUS ON THE WORK, NOT THE INDIVIDUALS

My final piece for the tool kit is to advise you to avoid personalizing the work to the extent possible. We tend to quickly personalize the triumphs and the failures, pointing the finger, and saying, "It is [fill in the blank with a person or an agency]'s fault that we are where we are today." We will all do better as we struggle to move our communities forward if we try to understand why something worked or did not, rather than pin the blame on the leader. People will constantly try to personalize the work. It is the leader's job to attempt to reframe the message and remove the individual from the attack.

As we have discussed earlier, people and agencies are naturally threatened by change. One great way to try to avoid the work of change is to take out the leader and hope things will go back to the way they used to be (Heifetz, 1994). This is where "thick skin" comes in, because as the leader you will invariably be tagged as the reason why something did not work out.

Moving Forward: Time to Dive In

If you choose to pursue leadership as part of your life's work, understand that it is a journey. There is no destination point. Leadership is a continual learning process. While you should take the opportunity to enjoy and savor success in your work as a leader, know that, in many cases, we learn more from our imperfections and failures than we do from our triumphs. In today's complicated world it is a tremendous responsibility to be a leader. You will survive only if you are doing it because you want to make a positive difference in the lives of people. Any lesser goal will ultimately lead to failure, as the road will be too difficult for those in it solely for personal gain.

We need solid, knowledgeable, and disciplined leaders working to create a positive future for vulnerable children and their families. Your reward for stepping out on behalf of your community will be measured by the number of children who someday will come to understand that if it hadn't been for your efforts in concert with your community, they might not be there with you to say thanks.

REFERENCES

Belasco, J.A. & R.C. Stayer (1993).
Flight of the Buffalo. New York: Warner Books.

Daloz, L.A., C.H. Keen, J.P. Keen & S.D. Parks (1996).
Common Fire: Leading Lives of Commitment in a Complex World. Boston: Beacon Press.

Edelman, M.W. (1999).
Lanterns: A Memoir of Mentors. Boston: Beacon Press.

Heifetz, R.A. (1994).
Leadership without Easy Answers. Cambridge, MA: Harvard University Press.

Heifetz, R.A. & M. Linsky (2002).
Leadership on the Line. Cambridge, MA: Harvard University Press.

CHAPTER SIX:

COMMUNITY SUCCESSES—

LISTENING AND ACTING

*As for the best leaders,
the people do not notice their existence.
When the best leaders' work is done,
the people say, "We did it ourselves."*

—Lao Tzu

One Saturday morning when I lived in Burlington, Vermont, three little children came up to my door and said, "Are you Mr. De Carolis, our city councilor?" And I said, "Yes." "Well, we have a petition for you." "Great!" I said, "What's the petition?" It turned out to be a request that a stop sign be put at the end of their street so the children could be safe as they crossed back and forth. "That is absolutely wonderful," I said. "I'll tell you what we're going to do with your petition. Come with me this Monday night to present it to the traffic commission; we'll try and get that stop sign for you."

So that's what we did. After school on Monday I gathered them up, and we went to meet the traffic commissioners. I don't think that group had ever had three young people show up at any of their meetings, which were held in the basement of the library. In fact, no one goes to those meetings. The three youngsters presented their petition, and I stood there with them. They got to see how the process worked. Three or four weeks later, they had their stop sign. *Listening . . . acting.*

The most important part of my work for six years as a city councilor was going once a month to a sixth-grade classroom where I had the teacher pick out two students to talk with me about how government works at the local level. They would come to the city council meeting at night. One time I took the class a newsletter on innovations in local government that comes out quarterly. As the two students were flipping through it, they spotted something that described "Kids' Day" in Seattle, Washington. Why couldn't we do something like that in Burlington, they asked? And I said, "Why not? Go ahead and draw up a resolution to present to the city council." So they did just that and presented it that night at the council meeting. It was passed thirteen to nothing. This past

Saturday, Burlington had its twentieth annual "Kids' Day."
Listening . . . acting.

What we know about communities also works in the field of children's mental health. Really look at each child and family, and then individualize care around them. Look at their strengths, find out the things they really like to do, and bring all the people who are important in their life (a teacher, a neighbor, family members, and various professionals such as psychiatrists, psychologists, clinical social workers, and others) around the table and come up with a plan. The magic that happens when we do that is profound. Clinical gains are enormous when young people are seen as individual human beings with individual needs that are addressed within a coordinated plan. Here is another situation where we have listening first . . . followed by action.

We also know that cities and towns are creatures of states—political subdivisions, if you will. We have city governments, county governments, and state governments. And they are not islands unto themselves. What makes magic happen is interconnectiveness—that child in that neighborhood in that city within that county and in that state, all working together. If we do that—if we have a state government that chooses to go out and listen to communities and hear what they need, we will see great things happen. We will see statutes written and implemented. We will see budgets that really respond to the needs of communities. We will see active and vibrant communities in a particular state or territory, or a Native American tribe articulating its interests to the country. We will see life from top to bottom, and bottom to top.

There is one more player in all of this, and that is the federal government. Back in the 1980s the federal government began to listen to Americans and to realize clearly that we were not effectively addressing the mental health needs of children. In those years, we were not listening, and then we began to listen in a new way. One of the tests that shows whether or not you are listening (and I put that test to you today) is to ask if what is being planned is relevant to those for whom the plan is made.

Starting twenty years ago, one of the things that was done was creating a vision of what life could be if we addressed the mental health needs of America's children in this new and different way. We talked about involving families. We talked about making all child-serving agencies come together to work on behalf of children. We talked about community systems that are culturally competent in the way they deliver services, in what services are built, in where the services are offered, and in the way these services reflect whatever it is that mental health means to different cultures in this wonderful country. We talked about focusing on the strengths of children. We talked of individualizing services. We talked about community as the place where all services could be delivered. And we agreed that we would end forever the notion of exporting children outside their home communities to get what they need. (Even though we knew quite well that the third biggest stress in life is moving, we still were moving kids all over the place to address their mental health needs.)

Lastly in this vision we talked about accountability—that whatever we did, whatever services we delivered, whatever systems we built, we would do it in a way that collected data so that we could go to a state legislature, a city council, a county council, or the federal government, and say: "Here's what we have done. Here's what it cost. And here are the outcomes of the work we are doing." That is the vision.

Now my guess is that this vision sits fairly well with all of you. I believe that this is what America wants. And we crafted this vision because first we *listened* and then we *acted*.

For nine years I was proud to steward a program at the federal level—some $100 million, which is small by federal standards. Yet this initiative is very powerful, I believe, in its capacity to help communities go through that process, with the help of their counties and states and with the federal government as their partner, to make life different for children who have mental health disorders, to give them a chance to have their strengths be actualized and their individual needs met, and to be a part of their own communities.

In the old days we used to talk about children and say, "This is a mental health child. No, this is an education child. No, this is a child welfare child, or a juvenile justice child." Well, the new mantra in the listening process is that these are our community's children. If we do that, then community works, the state works, and this country works.

So that's my message today about community successes. It is not about one community. It is about all of us in America, wherever we live, working together on behalf of children.

CHAPTER SEVEN:

LEADERSHIP FROM THE INSIDE OUT—

LESSONS LEARNED ABOUT SYSTEMS OF CARE

It is common sense to take a method and try it. If it fails, admit it frankly and try another, but above all try something.

—Franklin Delano Roosevelt

It has been nearly twenty years since I began work in systems of care. Hard to believe! What started in 1985 as a conversation with Rik Musty, a University of Vermont psychology professor and fellow Burlington City Council member, evolved into a seven-year stint at the Vermont Department of Mental Health, where I eventually became director of children's mental health, a nine-year tenure as the chief of the Child, Adolescent and Family Branch, Federal Center for Mental Health Services (CMHS), and now to leading a consulting firm devoted to expanding and strengthening systems of care. It has been a time filled with many triumphs and challenges and, at this point, I hope an America better able to address the mental health needs of our children and families.

When I started at the Vermont Department of Mental Health in 1985, my job was to oversee a five-year, $125,000-per-year federal strategic planning grant awarded from the branch I later led. Seven years later, I was heading up the branch and managing a budget that, by the time I left, was more than $100 million at the federal level, most of it committed to system-of-care efforts in communities and states throughout the country. There have been many lessons along the way, some painful, but most of them instrumental in helping a small federal grant program become an engine that has inspired thousands of people to work differently on behalf of children. Here are some of those lessons.

LISTENING

One of the early lessons that has stood me well throughout my career has been to listen to the hopes and dreams of all people involved in this work. From my early work in Vermont, where I developed a set of questions for parents of children with mental health disorders and for professionals from child-serving agencies, to surveying potential customers of technical assistance at the national level when I moved to Washington DC, listening has always been the essential ingredient for developing a vision that captured people's best sense of what could truly make a difference for their children and themselves. Needs assessments, phone calls, "town hall" style meetings, advisory boards, questionnaires, interviews, and focus groups are some ways that information can best be brought forward by people closest to the issues.

THE CHANGE PROCESS

Change within organizations and systems that have long done business a certain way comes slowly and not without conflict, loss, and some pain. It is relatively simple to identify barriers and changes that need to be made to markedly improve both process and outcomes, especially once you have canvassed people about what they want for their system. It is quite another matter to actually undertake the changes necessary to begin realizing the dreams.

There are so many variables that go into the change process. Is the right leadership in place to guide the change? Does the lead organization want to delay change even if others might see it as necessary? Are the staff members standing in the way of change even though they advocated for it at one time? Is the political climate right for change to take place? Is there a strategic plan designed to make the change occur in a way that is least intrusive to the staff and organization(s) involved? There is much food for thought here, but one must take care not to wait too long to weigh the risks before starting out, as things might CHANGE!

Gauging What Is Doable

An important lesson that we all need to learn is to keep the dreams of others, as well as our own visions of the possible, in proportion to what we can reasonably deliver with the personal and professional resources available. Those who neglect this "reality" factor find that it will interfere with both their professional and personal lives. In committing ourselves to work for better opportunities for children with serious emotional disturbance and their families, too many tend to overextend themselves, at times robbing themselves of a meaningful personal life and a manageable professional one. Working to scale is the critical issue here; taking careful stock of what you have to work with at any given time is paramount to successful systems change. If you are not good at gauging whether you are overextended, ask a few friends who care about you. Don't be surprised at what you hear.

The Business of Professional and Parent Relationships

In chapter 4, I wrote about the varying expectations of professionals versus parents. Working out the often complex relationship between these two groups is crucial to effective system-of-care work; it requires considerable effort to build and maintain successful partnerships. It is safe to say that families notice and appreciate any and all efforts on the part of professionals to develop positive parent/professional relationships. Many family organizations and individual parents come to the table with very little support from anyone other than family members in similar situations.

Difficulties often arise when professional/parent relationships are formalized through contracts or grants. The contracting relationship, initially viewed by all parties as a step forward and intended to financially solidify the relationship can easily begin a process of differing expectations that leads to mistrust and strained relationships. The "business" of the relationship can be a difficult concept for both family members and professionals to come to grips with within the work. Yet if this notion of business is not addressed and the relationship remains a "personal" matter, it is likely to rise and fall on what each can do for the other, rather than both sides coming to understand that contracts are about what work needs to be done and how. Contracts operate outside of personal relationships. See chapter 4 for more details.

The Importance of Supportive Work Environments

Real and lasting system change occurs in organizations that support system change agents in their work. In my case, on my first day of work in the Vermont Department of Mental Health, the division director said to me, "Gary, we are looking for you to lead us forward on children's mental health." What a wonderful invitation this was for me to launch my career of encouraging, creating, supporting, and even fomenting system change, first in Vermont, and then throughout the country on behalf of children with serious emotional disturbance and their families.

This experience sharply contrasts with another I had. Within a month of my arrival at that management position, my supervisor took me aside and informed me, "My job is to clip your wings." The comment was soon followed up by his demand that I show my daily schedule for his approval, which I refused to do. Little did I know that this kind of comment and action would be echoed time and again throughout my tenure at that position.

The contrast between these two opening comments is glaring. In order to do the difficult work of system reform you will need the support and trust given in the former example. Trying to lead an effort when you do not have the support of your organization's leadership is difficult at best. Before you go too far committing to an organization where you do not have the management's full faith and support, I recommend a long walk with a friend to think it over.

In some offices, and in some cases throughout entire organizations, one is struck by the general unhappiness of the staff. There may be a general sense of malaise and dispiritedness, and most staffers seem almost depressed. In other places, everyone from secretaries to the top managers exudes energy and excitement, the staff is happy and engaged with its work, and there is a strong feeling of a team all pulling together. In places like this, workers often eat lunch together, birthdays and other occasions are celebrated, and staffs come to the aid of a colleague who is distressed for one reason or another. When there is a tight deadline or a minor crisis, all pitch in to make it through the difficult patch. Certainly there are problems, but an overall sense of shared mission and camaraderie exists.

Why is the mood so different from one organization to another? Though it is hard to pinpoint the precise reasons, it appears that in organizations and groups that are not functioning well, people work as individuals rather than as a team. Staff lacks the sense that the individual's vision is important to the organization; if a staff person does have a vision to contribute there tends to be no vehicle for and maybe no interest in having that vision expressed to the organization's leadership. The work crunch is also often brutal. A crisis mentality of "we need this information yesterday" pervades the agency.

When you talk to the staff of organizations that are not functioning well, people by and large seem to be "doing time." There are exceptions to be sure, but over time those lights of vision seem to dim. Rumors, power grabs, and blaming of others seem to be the prevailing way of life. People are not inspired to do their best; rather, the environment seems to support "getting by," and talent is wasted.

The goal of creating an exciting, dynamic organization that honors field experience, diverse voices and an action agenda can be realized even within a larger agency that is functioning poorly. However, for the leader trying to create this dynamic operation, realizing this goal can bring the disdain of many inside the agency rather than support and acknowledgment for work well done. This lack of support, and even open opposition from some within the organization, can be hugely wearing over time.

My lesson learned is to read the messages that are being communicated to you in your work by the organization. Be yourself, do what you think is right, and judge if your approach and activities will be supported in your workplace. Work in a supportive environment! It is critical. Do not let your vision get in the way of finding a supportive work environment.

THE POWER OF MONEY

Surprise! The introduction of money changes the way people relate to each other. It also has the power to move people away from values and principles focused on children and families and introduce other values that have more to do with power and influence. Probably the most significant disappointment for me in Washington was to see how money dictated so much of what was done or not done, who you partnered with, how the basic tenets of a system of care could be so easily forgotten. How money is used to influence and bolster one's sense of self, how money replaces what needs to happen for children, and how relationships are built around securing and holding on to money are all sad realities in today's system-of-care work.

Don't get me wrong: I understand how important adequate funding is to the work we want to do and the goals we hope to accomplish, and that effort must be spent on obtaining financing. But it is a grave error to compromise principles of collaboration, integrity, and the focus on children and their parents for the sake of money. I fear that this kind of compromise has been made too often as federal funding for system-of-care development has grown. What I experienced are organizations that have chosen to live and die by federal contracts, but I have also seen that the introduction of significant new federal funding into communities—where resources have previously been scarce—contributed to enormous conflicts and divisiveness, with many people left bruised by the experience.

My one piece of advice for improving the chances that an influx of additional funds will be a positive factor in building systems of care is to adopt a strategy similar to what we developed in Vermont regarding children's individualized service planning. First, bring the family and relevant providers together to determine what services and supports are needed, leaving money totally out of the discussion. Once the need has been defined, move on to talk about what resources are needed and how to obtain them. Creating distance from the money by first clarifying what you want to accomplish and separating the service needs from the funding can help tame the power of money.

Find and Hold On to Your Sanctuaries

No matter how much you enjoy your work, do not treat it as the end all and be all in your life. Give yourself permission to enjoy life's pleasures, with the understanding that taking time out from work will make you a more effective leader. Make sure that you have many other life pursuits. Family, friends, hobbies, volunteer work, and other interests are critical to keeping you and your work alive.

Heifetz and Linsky (2002) speak to the importance of taking time for your "sanctuaries" to provide "reflection and renewal." This becomes difficult at times when you work within an organization that supports tight deadlines and understaffing of activities, with a culture that encourages overwork and views a balanced work effort in a negative light. If you have the inclination to pour yourself into work and are working in this kind of environment, you are asking for trouble over time. Fight the temptation—say "no" to ridiculous requests that leave no time for anything but work and say "yes" to taking care of yourself.

Many of us engaged in building community-based systems of care are driven to make sure that positive change happens and approach the work with a sense of mission. Outside activities are even more important to avoid burnout and sustain a sense of excitement and passion about the work. We must keep in mind that there is life beyond our jobs. The notion of taking care of yourself first before you can go out and be an effective change agent is so important. It takes a sense of faith and trust in yourself to do this, but with maturity, I have learned how important it is to rely on oneself when facing tough challenges.

For too many people, the lack of sanctuaries plays into the rush for an answer to relieve the anxiety of life's ambiguities. We need time to reflect, to heal, and to take care of ourselves, especially in tough times. Sanctuaries can serve this purpose. Ignoring the need for time away from the work leads to many false starts, as the hoped-for quick answer is not, in the end, usually the path best suited to achieve one's goals.

STEADY AND CONSISTENT LEADERSHIP

When I look at successful communities, as well as my own leadership experiences, maintaining consistent, stable leadership has been a key factor in enabling change to move forward in a consistent way. As leaders and staff grow and change, they do so within a culture that has been laid down over time. It allows them to take some risks, knowing what the community rules of the game are. A frequent turnover in leadership almost inevitably leads to fits and starts, with very little progress made in the communities where I have seen this occur. If someone considering a leadership position does not want to make a long-term commitment, I counsel this person to seriously rethink whether he or she should even apply for the leadership position, given the negative impact a short-term stay is likely to have on the staff and system.

Another aspect of leadership consistency is grooming the next leader within your organization. In the business community, a recent survey revealed that 72 percent of chief executive officers were grooming the leader who would take their place. How many of us in leadership roles in the public sector are mentoring the next leader? It is a professional obligation as part of being a leader to help prepare those who have the aptitude and interest to learn the skills of leadership. Start mentoring.

FRIENDSHIPS

It is safe to say that, in the end, leaders have very few people in their work world who could be considered close friends—the kind that will stand up for you through thick and thin. This is only to be expected. The leadership position is so laden with power issues, and it is vital for leaders to understand that even if you think you have a close friend in someone with whom you also have a working relationship, the friendship is always suspect, given the power of your position. This is true whether the friendship is between the leader and his or her direct staff, or with a person who somehow relies on the leader for resources, access, or authority. Times of turmoil usually clarify who truly cares about the leader as a person and who is more interested in what power that leader has through his or her position. Heifetz (1994) offers an insightful look at the difference between allies and confidants.

Though it may sound trite, it is crucial that you be your own best friend. This means that you make sure you are doing the things in life and work that make you feel good. Be driven by your inner values, purposes, and sense of self rather than by the job or pressure from someone else. This can be tough and it tests your ability to put your own well-being first, but it is so important. When you think of coming to the aid of a close friend, you know you would do anything for that person, right? Well, you also need to "do anything" for yourself! How many of us think that way? And how many actually act on this, making ourselves top priority, particularly in times of stress?

RUMORS AND GOSSIP

The gossip mill is intriguing. What can seem like innocent chatter can be so damning to the leader. I remember in one state, staff in the system of care referred to gossip as "the coconut line." If someone wanted to damage the leader, he or she would start a rumor. Share a damning tale that includes a grain of truth but is far from the whole story, and off it goes. The pain this inflicts on the leader and the system is tremendous. Rumors can stop the change process, which is the goal of the rumormonger in the first place.

Rumors crop up most often when a leader is pushing for change or when change is under way and is threatening the status quo. Spreading a rumor is a passive and quite insidious way to protest something that a party does not want to change. There's no clear method of dealing with rumors. In my experience, the best thing to do is anticipate that rumors will happen and continue what you are doing. Avoid giving in to the negative distraction of unfounded allegations; yet defend yourself if they reach a formal level or if you have a chance to directly confront the person responsible for the rumor. Conversely, do not ever participate in them yourself. In fact, if you hear someone spreading a rumor, speak up and tell him or her that you feel uncomfortable talking about another person that way. Given all the work of building a system of care, we must have better things to do with our time.

Empower Your Staff

It is clear to me that the primary role of the leader is to help staff become the best they can. Modeling and offering opportunities to grow and learn while working on the day-to-day tasks is critical. Having discussions about what is working for them and how they can do better at their work is key, yet we too often become so immersed in myriad workday activities that it is hard to find time for teaching or guidance.

The challenge for leaders is how to foster this culture in a very busy office. Strategies might include using staff meetings more effectively, with specific goals related to staff skill-building and growth; perhaps taking time for one-on-one walks outside during the lunch hour; or even using the walk to the lunchroom or coffee shop as a chance to share and mentor. The employee appraisal system can certainly be used as a chance for staff to learn and grow. A simple question with profound implications that brings us back to the beginning of this chapter is: How can the leader listen more and talk less?

These steps are easy to write about but can be very difficult to implement when all the action of a busy office gets rolling. If the leader fails to pay attention to staff development issues, they are likely to end up very low on the priority list, which will prove to be a detriment to individual staff as well as the entire organization over the long term.

Sustaining Systems of Care in Tough Times

Institutionalizing gains made in building systems of care is crucial, lest they be seen as one-time demonstrations that need not be continued. The country is in a recession, and federal and state tax cuts have shrunk the budgets of most states and the nonmilitary parts of the federal government. One of the fallouts has been cuts to children's mental health budgets in many states. Some of the states that have been most effective in building systems of care have seen a major shift in direction, resulting in the firing or resignation of successful leaders.

I recently spoke with the former director of children's mental health in a state where the implementation of systems of care was roaring along. Suddenly, with a new chief, the direction had changed and systems of care was not going to be the big-ticket item it had been. Everything became a push/pull dynamic; a job that had been a joy and brought a great sense of accomplishment was now a constant struggle and source of tension. Within weeks the director resigned. She told me that she was committed to making sure leaders embarking on system change understand how difficult it is to accomplish and sustain. Continuing the status quo is far more comfortable and appealing for most of us; people will usually resist change no matter how beneficial it may be for them and their customers.

Promoting policy development is an important way to protect systems of care in this time of flux. Where this has occurred on a statewide level, it has made some difference in ongoing support for systems of care. Also, this is a time when the need for interagency collaboration is crucial, so that the various child-serving departments are interdependent and less vulnerable to huge program and service cuts. If one department's budget is cut, another may be able to pick up the shortfall. For example, in one state the governor favored one child-serving agency over other departments. So, while one was being cut, the other was getting more money to carry out governor-initiated programs. Because the two departments worked together and had blended funds to create new services, the department that received new money was able to carry forward the programs that were cofunded. The financial load shifted a bit, but the integrity of the programs remained.

In communities where strong family organizations have been developed, parents of children with mental health needs can make a real difference in advocating not making any budget cuts on services to their children. If any of these pieces were not in place before the recession, it is hard to mobilize them at this late date.

TRAINING AS AN INVESTMENT

As I have read and thought about leadership and system change, I have become painfully aware of how little we are focused on those aspects of our work in the public sector and, more specifically, in community-based systems of care. We continue to try to infuse training activities into the culture of organizations, which in itself is difficult, as training is a nonbillable service under Medicaid. Likewise, the notion of leadership development as an activity is far removed from funding streams that are focused solely on the services to the client. I do not see anywhere near an equivalent focus on building a strong workforce in government or community organizations as exists in the business arena.

Given that few states pay for training as a part of the menu to their employees and that community organizations are always struggling for the dollars to survive, another funding source needs to be identified. Perhaps it is the role of the federal government to underwrite the kind of training and technical assistance needed to build strong leaders in the public sector. Perhaps state-level technical assistance centers could become the norm, versus the existing large national centers that are far removed from local issues. A grant program that would enable states to design their technical assistance and compete for money, and require them to provide matching funds to be eligible for an award would be a way to address this issue. Also, the national centers could mentor and train the state technical assistance centers on what it takes to be successful. California and Pennsylvania are leaders in this area.

INTERAGENCY COLLABORATION

Interagency collaboration is like mom and apple pie: we all take for granted that it is good and right. However, too often the concept is given lip service. A memorandum of understanding is developed, people from different agencies attend a few meetings together, or, perhaps, one organization hosts a training for another. But nothing really changes much at the client level.

Only when agencies and their leaders are willing to actually share some meaningful responsibilities and resources does interagency collaboration begin to take hold. This is when the real work of building a system of care for children and their families begins. The success of interagency collaboration requires initially giving more than one gets, which means taking some risks. As the collaboration process gets under way, the level of trust among would-be partners is usually quite low, while the fear of what one's agency might stand to lose through collaboration is quite high. I have found that a willingness to share grant dollars among agencies and encouraging other financial options for blending dollars can go a long way to help assuage fears and build trust among partners.

In children's mental health, we have been blessed with growing grant opportunities for building family organizations and systems of care. Using some of those funds to help one's sister agencies can be a great way to help build strong collaborative relationships. When departments of mental health keep all grant dollars within their control and give only lip service to sharing the grant benefits with their sister agencies, I have seen few if any collaborative relationships grow. We all need to give to get.

It seems obvious that including all relevant child-serving agencies in the collaborative process is the right thing to do. But this seldom happens, almost always to the detriment of the system-of-care development process. Given that people and organizations need time to get comfortable with interagency arrangements, it is important to have the whole team meet together even before it is clear what each role will be. Assembling the whole team early on will prevent the resentment that occurs if an agency is not included, or when they are invited later and know that "we were the last to be thought of."

All too often in our system-of-care work there are only two or three agencies that are really a part of the interagency process, and no parents. A system of care needs to involve all the child-serving agencies if it is to be successful for all children. State agencies should include: child welfare, mental health, developmental disabilities, special education and education, juvenile justice, health, substance abuse, vocational rehabilitation, the umbrella agency of human services and, if separate, the Medicaid office. Families need to be a part of any interagency structure and included as equal partners in decision-making. I recommend that at least three parents join the team. They need to be paid and accommodations made as to time of meetings so they can be active members. Parents add a depth of wisdom that will make a good idea become a great idea. They serve as an all-important reality check, bringing in practical, concrete suggestions and questions that professionals might miss.

CULTURAL COMPETENCE

Achieving cultural competence within systems of care is certainly doable, but it requires people to take risks and leave their comfort zones. The book *Common Fire* (Daloz, et al, 1996), which looks at a hundred successful social change leaders, found that for nearly all, a notable part of their background was an "out of tribe" experience early in life. This gave them the opportunity to expand their world view and see beyond their own ethnic or cultural norms. The experiences they had were simple: summer camp with children from other cultures, a family trip to another country, or visiting relatives in another part of the United States.

We can all have that experience. It is never too late. It has saddened me over the years to see communities that are rich with cultural diversity and then note that the staff members hired to work with those communities are so often limited to one race, usually white. Beyond the obvious prejudice issues that I know still exist, it's clear there is a lack of valuing and including the many cultures, races, and ethnic backgrounds of this country, and I have tried to understand what else is driving this.

Three factors work against our taking full advantage of the wealth of diversity we have in our communities today. First, there is a low level of trust between and among the races, classes, and cultural and ethnic groups in this country. Our history as a nation has eroded the ability of people to trust each other across these divides, especially as people of color think about relating to Anglo-Americans. Second, when it comes to opening oneself up to work and develop friendships with people from different cultures, there is incredible inertia. I am amazed that even as we claim to appreciate the importance of cultural competence, we will still hire a staff that almost solely represents the leader's race and cultural background.

I often tell the story of walking into a planning meeting for one system-of-care community some years back, looking around the room and being taken aback at the lack of family representatives and people of color. "How could this be?" I asked. I really had nothing against this group of bright, committed professionals, but they had missed two critical stakeholders for this meeting. It wasn't good enough for me to hear that they met with people of color, as well as family representatives, separately. That just harkened back to the "separate but equal" notion of years past.

My third observation speaks to fear. What will it mean if you disclose that you know very little about someone else's culture? What if you make a move that shows a lack of sensitivity or offends? What will it mean to people of my race if you choose to be with someone from another cultural or racial group? That great movie *Guess Who's Coming to Dinner* is still very relevant today!

Overcoming the formidable barriers facing us regarding cultural competence is, like building effective systems of care, all about taking risks and system change. This challenge provides a perfect metaphor for what we as individuals need to do. If we cannot move out of our comfort zones, taking the simple risk of inviting someone into our lives who is from a different class or race, and working together in diversity, than I fear that we cannot build systems of care. This is what Heifetz (1994) refers to as an "adaptive challenge."

I have faith that we can reach across these barriers, and I have seen it begin to happen. Several years back, the Center for Mental Health Services' Child, Adolescent and Family Branch held a national meeting in Puerto Rico on cultural competence for all communities in the process of building their systems of care. They invited representatives from US territories who wanted to learn from others about how to build systems. Some fifty communities shared their energy, commitment, and creativity around working toward culturally competent systems of care. We can do it. The time is now.

Another aspect of cultural competence is the technical side of the issue. What is good policy in cultural competence for provider organizations? How do we operationalize the principle of cultural competence so that it becomes part of the day-to-day operations of an organization? What are stellar training programs for new staff? How do we make sure that clinical practice and type and location of services are tailored to meet a community's various cultures? How do we gain consistent insight into the cultural needs of families? How do we celebrate culture within our systems of care? These and other questions need to be answered so that we create an infrastructure around cultural competence that is transferable across very different communities.

WATCH YOUR LANGUAGE

Within the new paradigm of interagency collaboration and involving families in all aspects of the work, how we use language becomes either a barrier to the effort or a vehicle to enhance the new partnerships we are creating. First and foremost, the use of "child first" language moves us all forward in seeing children as children first and then recognizing that they may have a disability, e.g., talking about "a child with a serious emotional disturbance" rather than using the label "a seriously emotionally disturbed child." When the disability is listed first, you lose the sense that this is, in fact, a child. Too often we see an even more extreme misuse of language, in which the child isn't even mentioned, as in "the seriously emotionally disturbed." This is like listening to nails on a chalkboard.

Almost as troublesome is the use of abbreviations and acronyms. There is no better way to disempower families than for professionals to use their jargon at meetings where families and other agencies are in attendance. No one understands the abbreviations except the "club members."

Not so long ago, I was teaching a graduate education class of future special educators, and when I mentioned this notion of avoiding abbreviations or acronyms one student quickly raised her hand. She was insulted by my remarks and said it is the family's duty to learn the terms, rather than making professionals say everything in whole words. Her classmates immediately took her to task for this response. I'm not sure she will be any different when she enters her field. I just hope that enough parents and professionals are sufficiently bold to help her see a different way of relating to others in her work. If we are to develop new working teams to create a system, we need everyone to make a real effort to speak the same language.

Use Your Data!

Hard data, made real by combining the numbers with parents' stories about the frustrations of trying to get services for their children, is one of the most powerful ways to reach the public, media outlets, advocates, and policy makers. Data need to be communicated in such a way that various audiences can understand. I found that having the project leader and evaluator share the communication role is powerful because each provides a different vantage point. Keeping the audience in mind and keeping the information simple, as opposed to overwhelming people with mind-numbing statistics, can go a long way in helping interested but uninformed key constituents better appreciate your efforts.

Data are not just something to be kept for internal purposes. Today no public agency or initiative can expect any legislative body's support unless it can demonstrate both good outcome data and high-quality data collection processes. This underscores the principle of accountability at all levels in systems of care.

By the way, ever since I began work in systems of care, I made sure that the lead evaluator's office was next to mine, so that I had ready access to the data and an expert who could run specific analyses for groups that I might be meeting with. It is that important.

Social Marketing

Here is another vehicle for the use of your system-of-care data. Many people in human services are afraid of the whole notion of marketing. I can remember that when I first entered the public sector, there was a prevailing sense that it was crucial to avoid press coverage of one's agency at all costs. If you follow that logic, what happens is that your agency will end up in the paper and on the evening news for negative incidents that are bound to occur over time, and the public never has a chance to see the great positive contributions you are making on an everyday basis.

Given that we operate in a market economy, whoever tells the most compelling story will usually catch the attention first of the public and then the legislature—the legislature will only go as far as the public will let it. Keeping the public ignorant is a sure way to keep the door locked on any support from the legislature. And legislative support is vital to sustainability over the long run.

Develop a social marketing plan and roll it out through a strategically planned approach. It is another part of the sustainability plan. Don't neglect to include the advocacy organizations in your state and community. In most cases, they will be able to tell your story and contact the media in ways that most government bureaucracies cannot.

FROM THEORY TO PRACTICE— THE STRUGGLES OF IMPLEMENTATION

Over the years, there has been a wealth of suggestions to enhance and improve systems of care. What we have learned is that an idea is only as good as the implementation strategy and the people who carry it out. When left to people who do not have the skill to implement them, even the best ideas quickly turn bad.

I would like to share an example. Based on a focus group and a telephone survey of grantees involved in the Comprehensive Community Mental Health Services for Children and Their Families Program, the notion of having "peer mentors" was adopted as a way to support growing systems of care. Peer mentors would be individuals working in system-of care communities who had developed expertise in building and maintaining a system of care. The mentors would not have to leave their current positions, as each was assigned only one or two grant communities, and could use the phone, e-mail, and an occasional site visit to do the necessary support work. Sounded like a good idea.

Unfortunately, it did not turn out well. Where the concept of peer mentors fell through was the implementation of a plan of action, including training and supervision of the peer mentors. What was missing? A step-by-step strategy was never developed, nor was a set of guidelines defining the peer mentor role. Training both peer mentors and the grant communities to understand how to maximize their relationship did not occur. And finally, supervision of the peer mentors was left unclear.

Lacking sufficient guidance and instruction, the mentors were left with their own ideas about how this should work. The more assertive mentors called the assigned grant communities, made contact, and built relationships with the appropriate people within the system of care. The less assertive in many cases did not make those calls or were initially rebuffed by the grant communities for various reasons and did not pursue them. The person assigned to oversee the whole operation had little authority and was in the role of a logistics coordinator rather than a content or process coordinator. Little attention was paid to developing the kinds of protocols and processes that would have made the most of the relationship.

The final complicating factor was the decision to have both a professional and a parent peer mentor for each grant community, based on the rationale that using parent/professional teams was an instructive model for grant communities. However, creating a prototype of how two mentors should work together while trying to deal with the dynamic of both holding the same position was just too much for such a new concept. The grant communities complained about not knowing whom to call for what, how difficult it was to get both peer mentors on the phone at the same time, having to repeat information when only one mentor was initially reached, coordinating two schedules for a community visit, and the like. The two-mentor approach also became a burden for the technical assistance center, whose budget supported this effort.

A simple idea and yet such a complicated story of missed opportunity. In the end, the peer mentors were not happy, the grant communities were not happy, and my branch, which over-saw the contract, was not happy. Lesson learned: ideas are only as good as the implementation strategy and the personnel assigned to carry it out. Better to have fewer ideas and focus one's time and effort on assuring their success than to have many great ideas without the capacity to effectively implement them.

Concluding Thoughts

The first job I had after my undergraduate work was as a counselor in a community-based correctional center in Newark, New Jersey. There was a sergeant of the correctional staff who obviously was a bright man and had much wisdom to share about his years in this field. He said something to me one day that I have always remembered, and that in some ways was the inspiration for this book. "Gary," he said, "You will experience a lot in your life, but unless you actually write down what you have learned it will be wasted. Be sure to capture the wisdom that you will develop in the written word so others can benefit from it. I only wish I had done this." So, as we end this book and this section on lessons learned, I suggest you do the same.

Experience life, make the most of your years in this work, and be sure to write it down so others can learn.

I leave you with some words of wisdom that I believe sum up my values and perspective about system change work better than any I could have written myself:

> *It is not the critic who counts; not the person who points out how the strong person stumbles, or where the doer of deeds could have done them better. The credit belongs to the person who is actually in the arena, whose face is marred by dust and sweat and blood; who strives valiantly; who errs, and comes short again and again; because there is not the effort without error and short-comings; but who does actually strive to the deeds; who knows the great enthusiasms, the great devotions; who spends himself in a worthy cause, who at the best knows in the end triumphs of high achievement and who at the worst, if he fails, at least fails while daring greatly, so that his place shall never be with those cold and timid souls who know neither victory nor defeat.*

—Theodore Roosevelt

REFERENCES

Daloz, L.A., C.H. Keen, J.P. Keen & S.D. Parks (1996).
Common Fire. Boston: Beacon Press.

Heifetz, R.A. (1994).
Leadership without Easy Answers. Cambridge, MA: Harvard University Press.

Heifetz, R.A. & M. Linsky (2002).
Leadership on the Line. Cambridge, MA: Harvard University Press.